AF594032

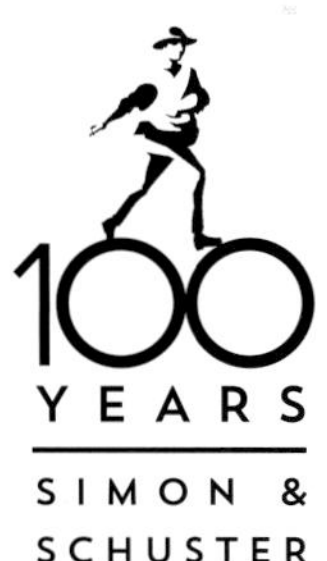
100
YEARS
SIMON &
SCHUSTER

THINGS SHOULDN'T BE SO HARD

BETH GARRABRANT

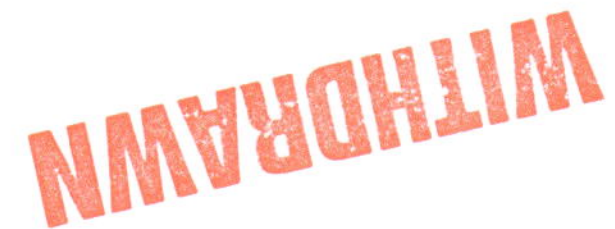

SIMON & SCHUSTER
New York London Toronto Sydney New Delhi

TIME TO KILL, TIME TO BURN

by Kelly Reichardt

Born in 1985, Beth Garrabrant was raised thirty miles north of Chicago in Lake Forest—a suburb made infamous in the 1980 film *Ordinary People*. Following in the deep footprints of the heavies before her—Robert Adams, Joel Sternfeld, Steven Shore, and William Eggleston—Garrabrant concerns herself with the American Midwest and those who dwell there.

Things Shouldn't Be So Hard is her first book and features photos shot between 2001 and 2017. Here we have one woman's take on an era beginning with the first days of George W. Bush's presidency, through the 9/11 attacks, the invasion of Iraq, economic collapse, eight years of Barack Obama, bank bailouts, right up to the swearing in of Donald J. Trump.

From Garrabrant's vantage point, all seems well in the heartland. Instead of a ruckus country on the brink of war with itself, here is a sense of continuity, the steady pulse of day-to-day living: a fair comes to town, a dance recital is approaching, swim practice is underway. Time seems expansive in a way that seems pre-internet or perhaps it's just the way it works when one is young and has time to kill, time to burn. The sense of an afternoon stretching out at the kitchen table, while a young woman, maybe home from college, listens to her brother play his French horn. At first glance, one might even get the impression these photos are from a bygone era. But on closer look: a teen is wearing a pair of Crocs, someone in the group is clutching a cell phone, the corner of a computer screen cuts into the frame.

Garrabrant's photos pleasantly leave a lot of space and openness for us to bring our own baggage. For instance, a stairway in a school hallway with an inspirational message painted on each step. Should one make it from "I won't do it" to "Yes, I did it!" they would be able to find out what's on the pink and yellow flyers taped to the walls at the top of the stairs. Personally, I see an empty school hallway and immediately think of a crime scene. I wonder if the kids are still cowering in the corner of their rooms. But is that dark undercurrent there? I show the photo to a friend and ask her what she sees: "I was in a high school stairwell like that when I told my best friend I was pregnant."

I wonder if the long-haired kid behind register Number One is a fan of Dinosaur Jr.

What's worse than your mother and her boyfriend making out in a hot tub four feet away from you?

The young girls in power suits and pearls scare me a bit.

The woman on the Rascal scooter sure seems to be in a hurry. No one else is in sight, the area is sprawling, I imagine she's got a ways to go. I hope her battery holds out.

Everywhere you look—ordinary people.

Kelly Reichardt is a writer and director whose films include *Showing Up*, *First Cow*, *Certain Women*, *Night Moves*, *Meek's Cutoff*, *Wendy and Lucy*, *Old Joy*, and *River of Grass*.

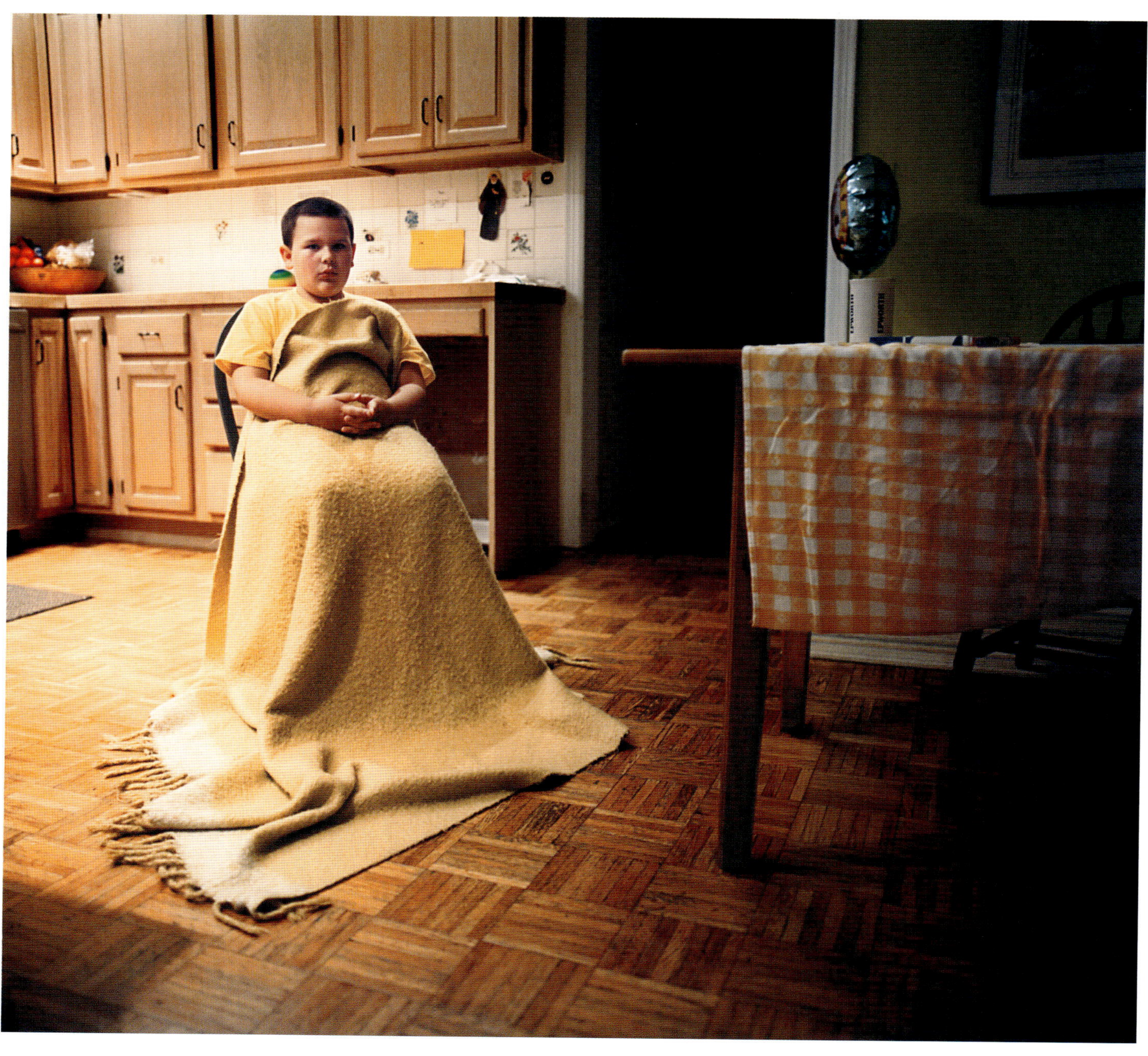

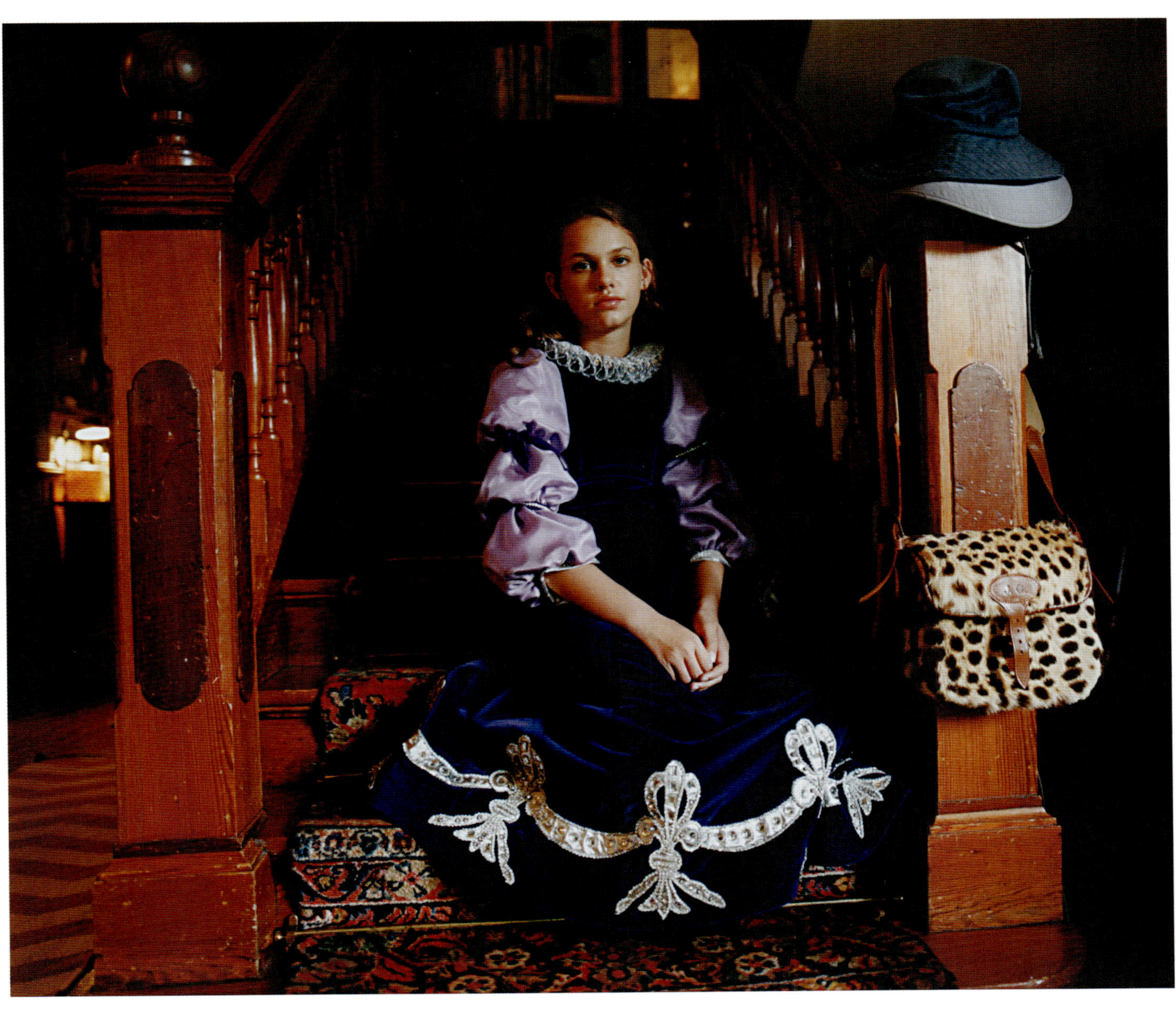

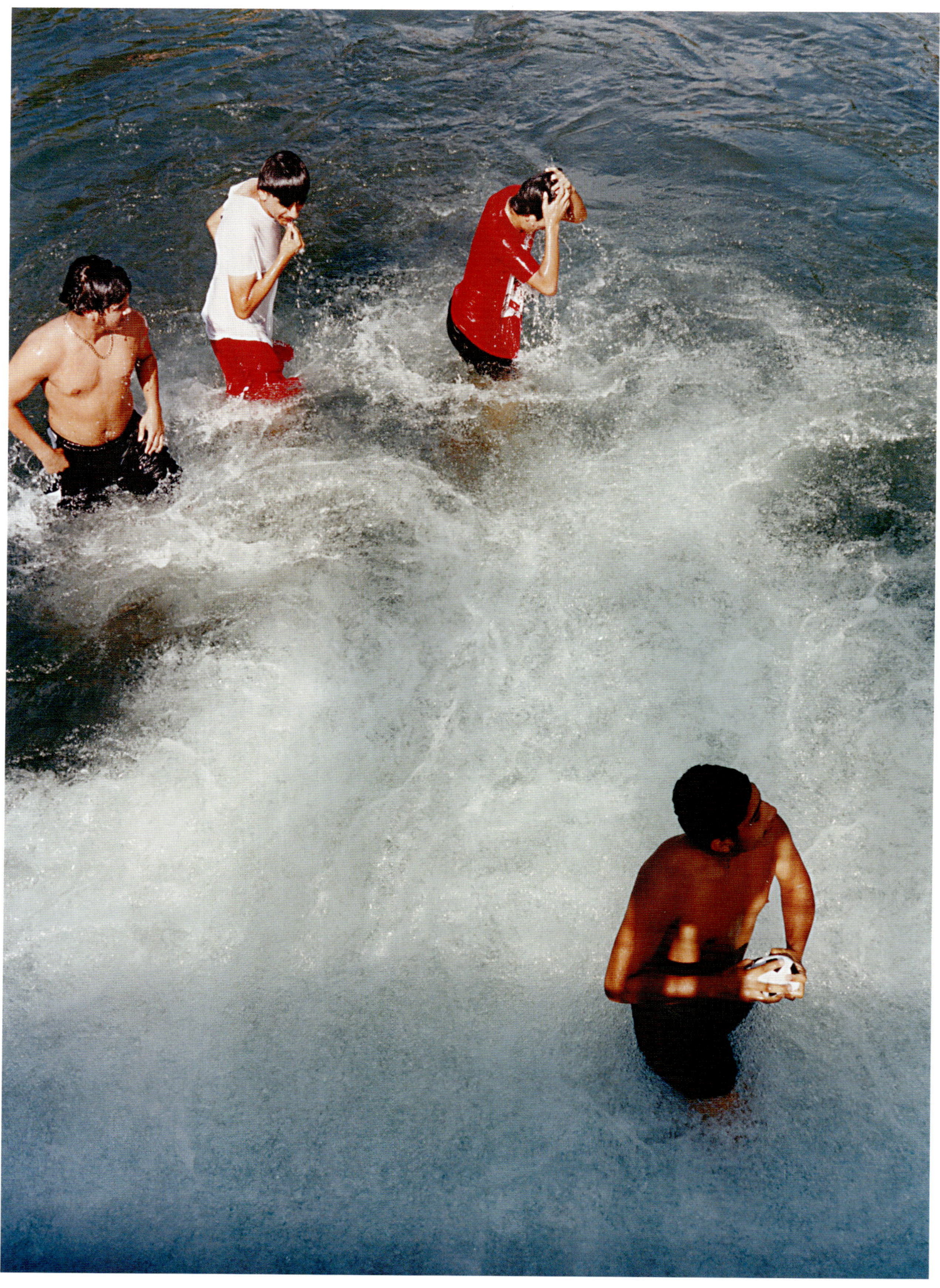

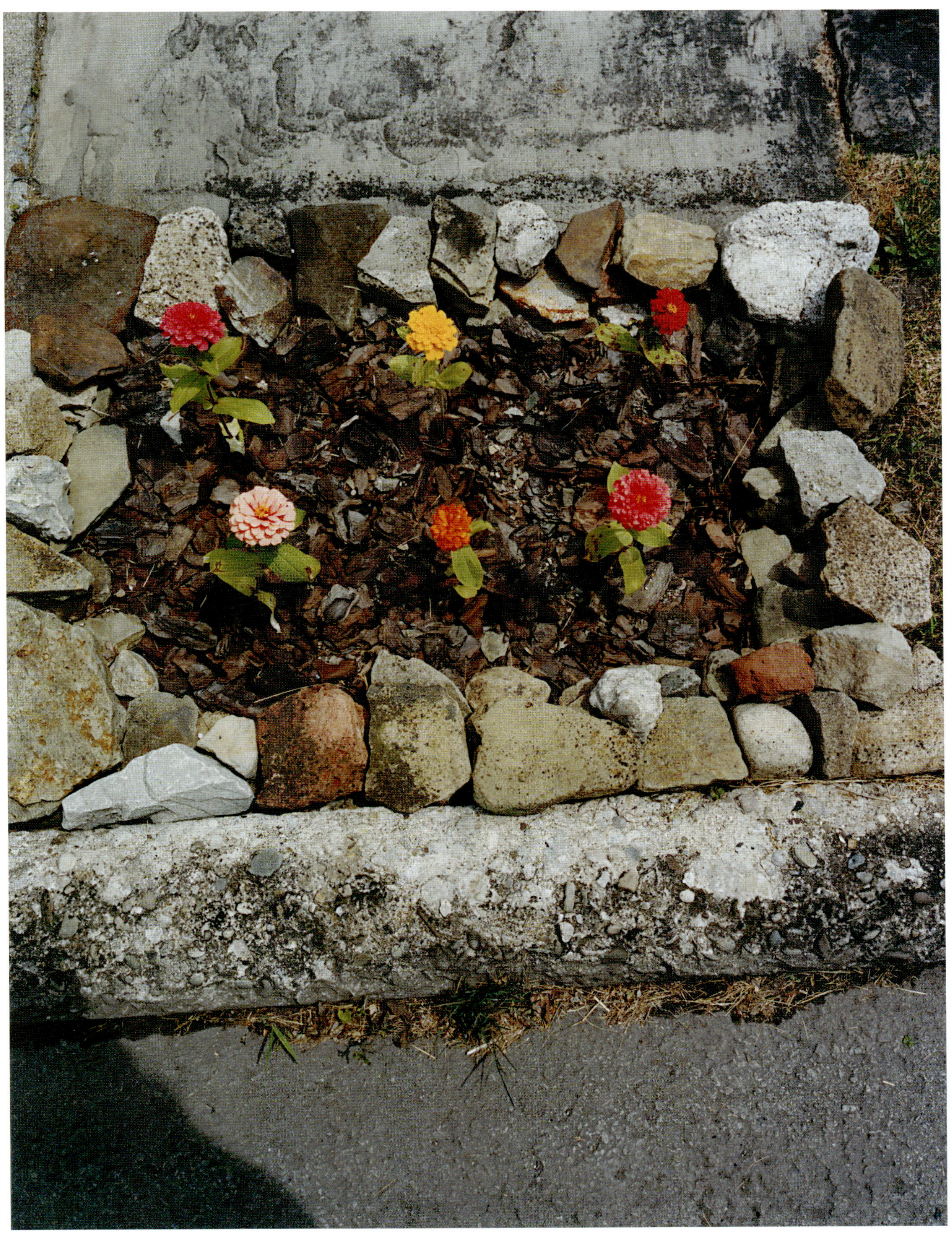

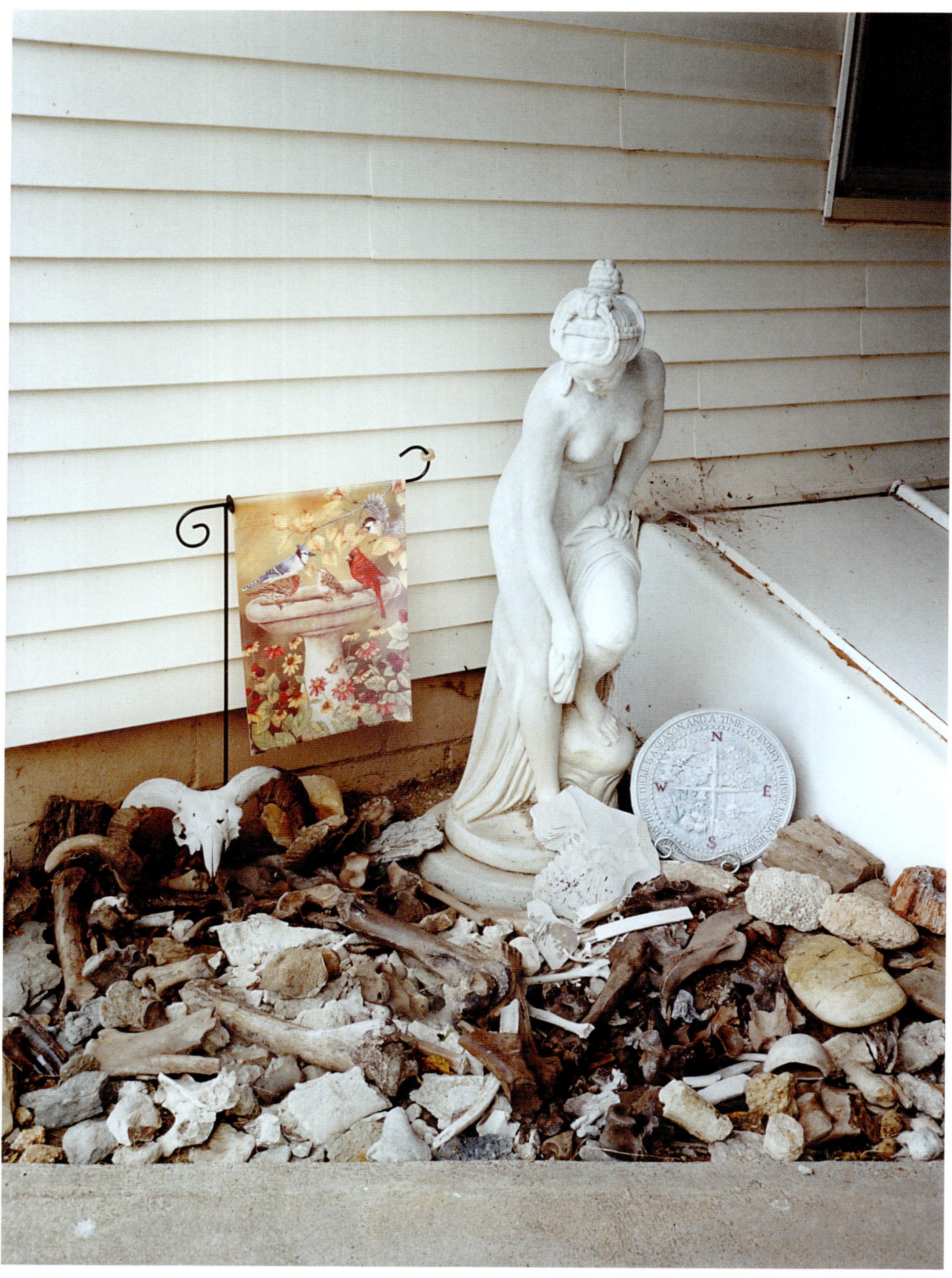
THERE IS A SEASON AND A TIME TO EVERY PURPOSE UNDER HEAVEN
N
W
E
S

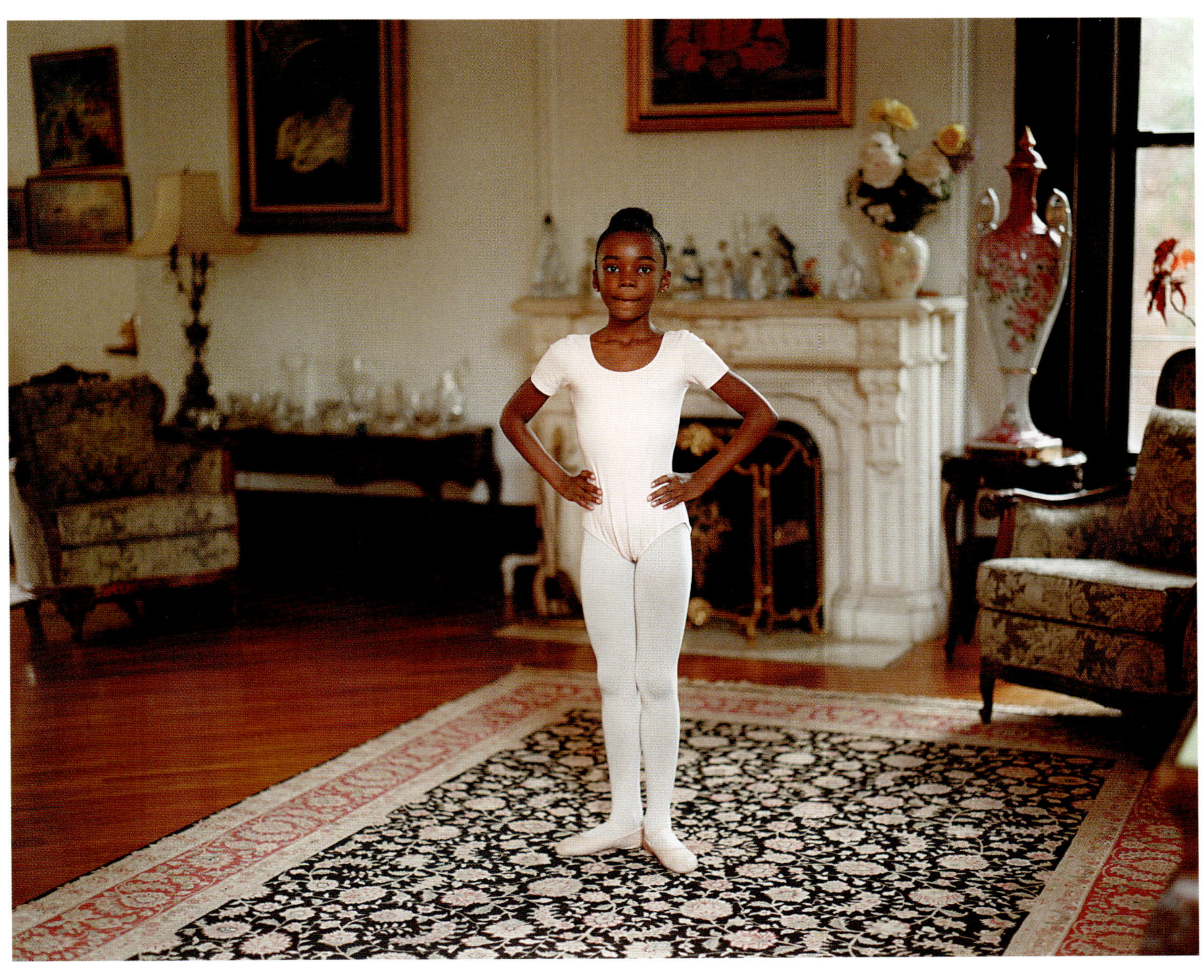

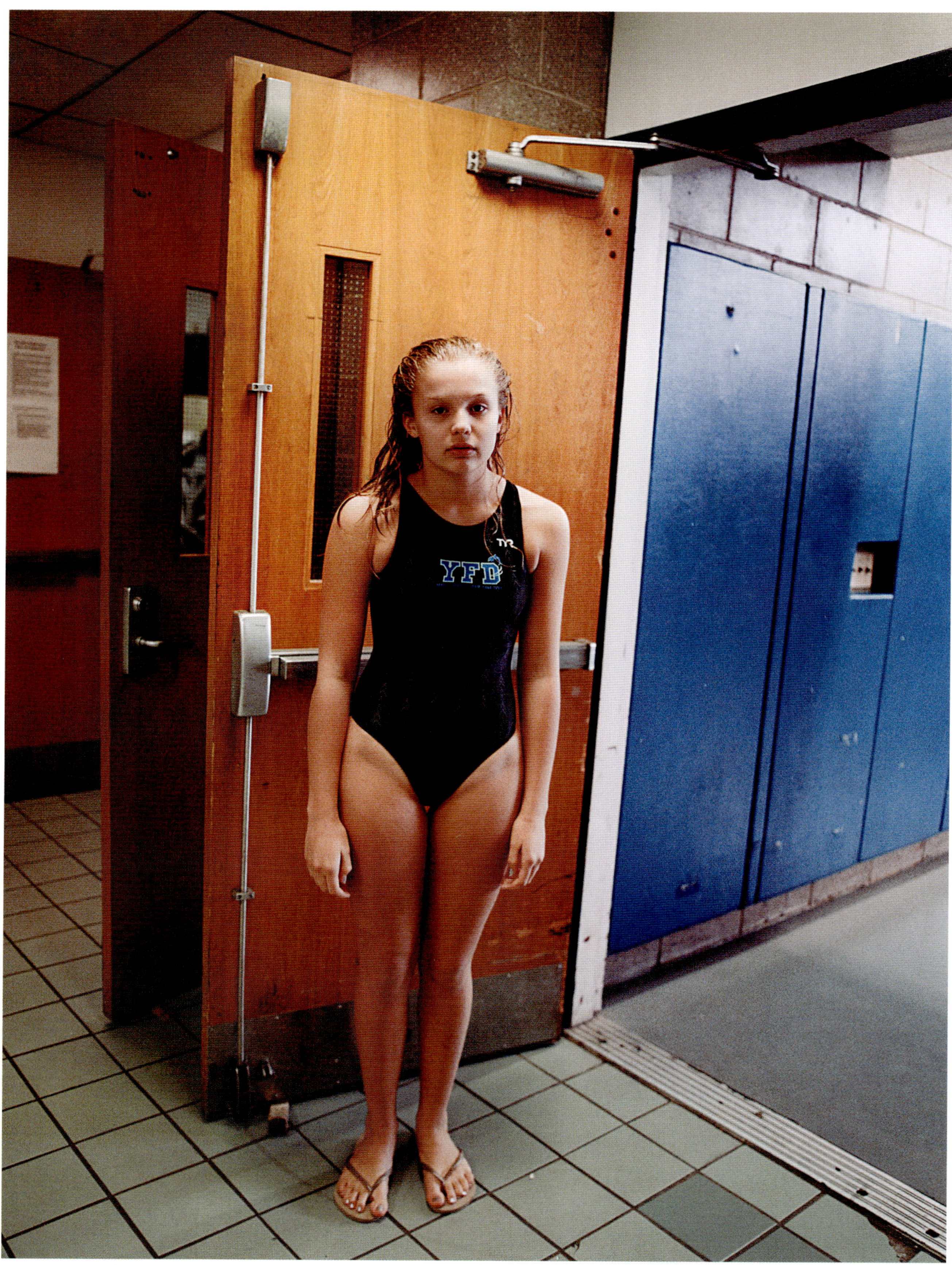
YFD

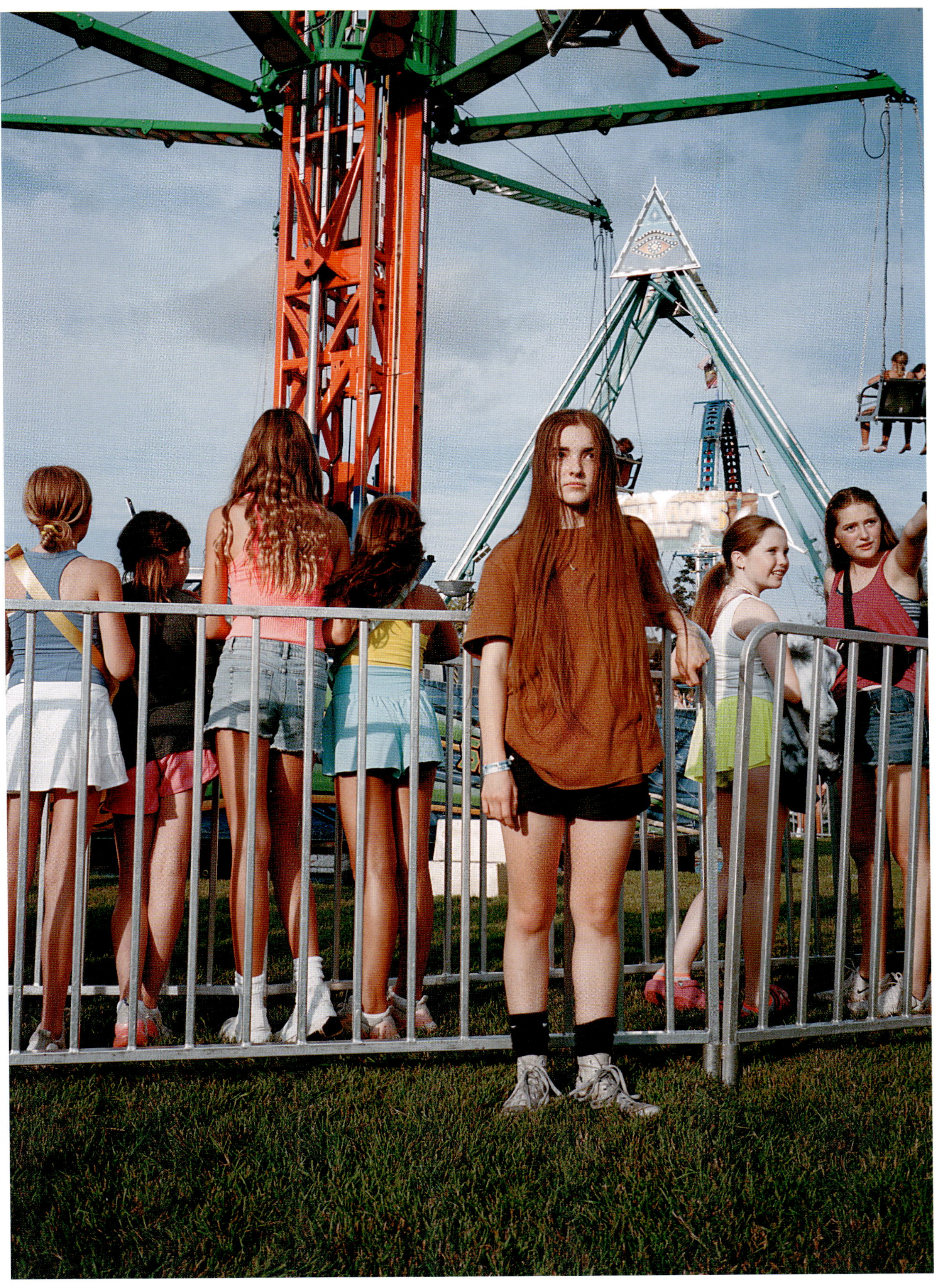

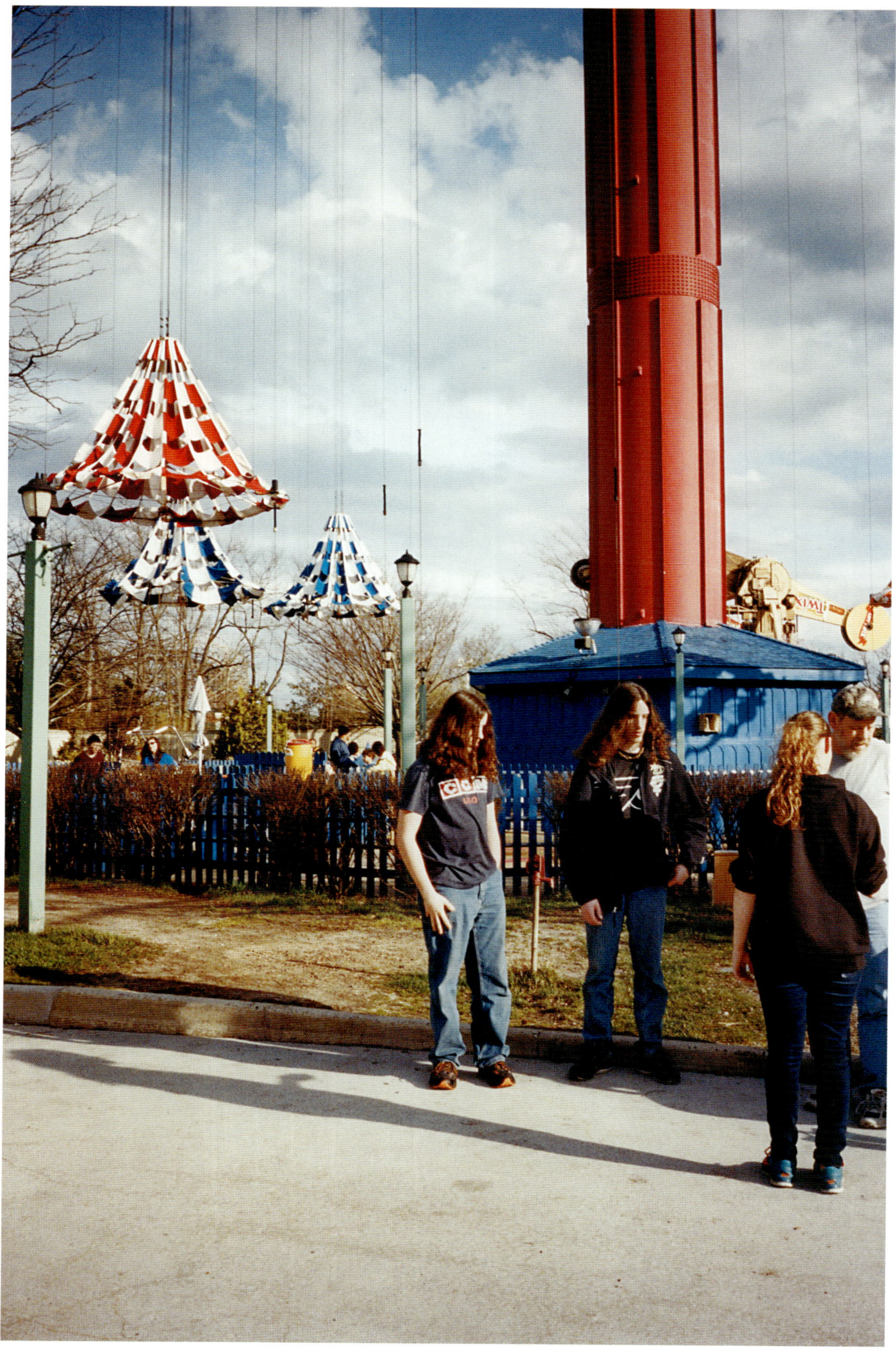

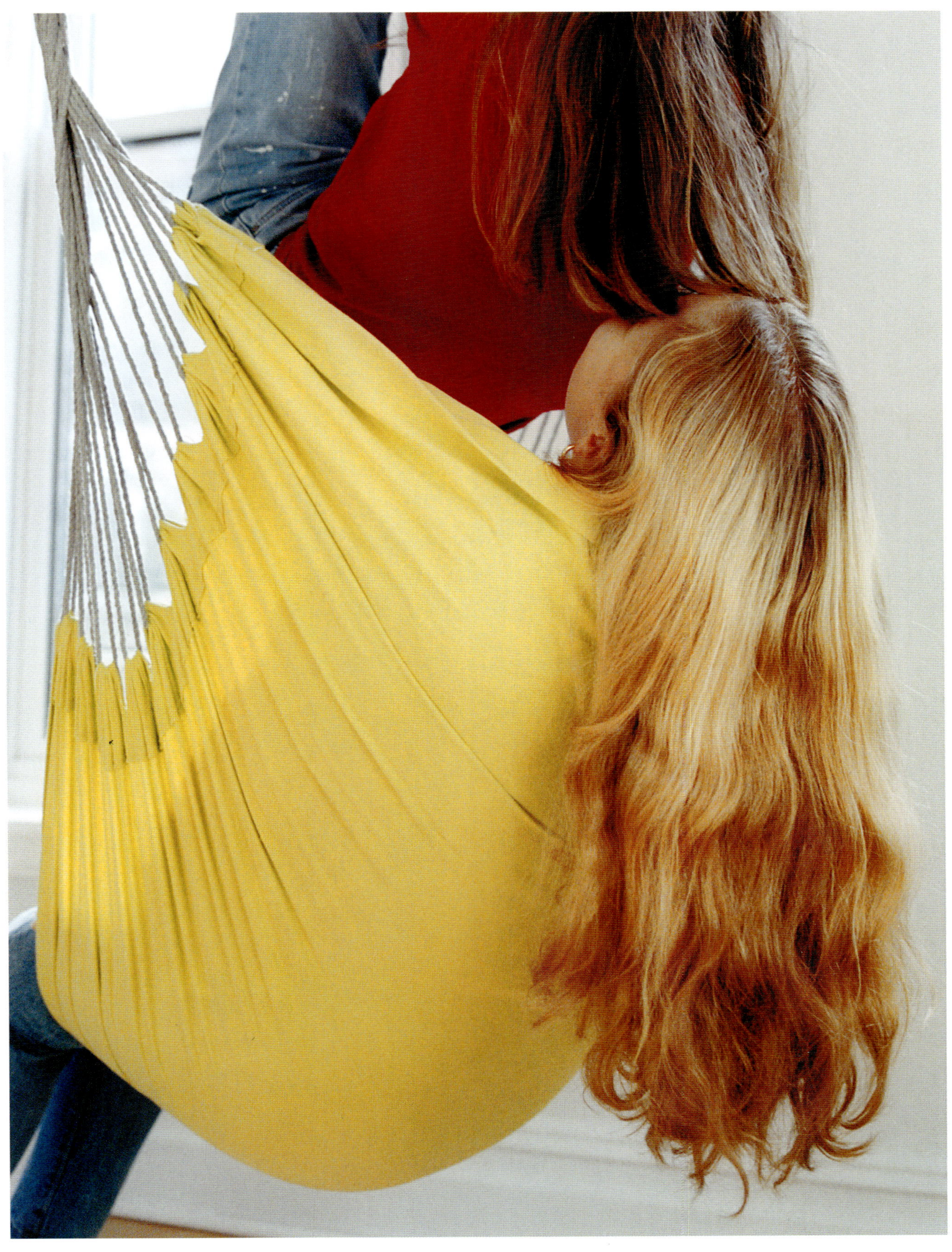

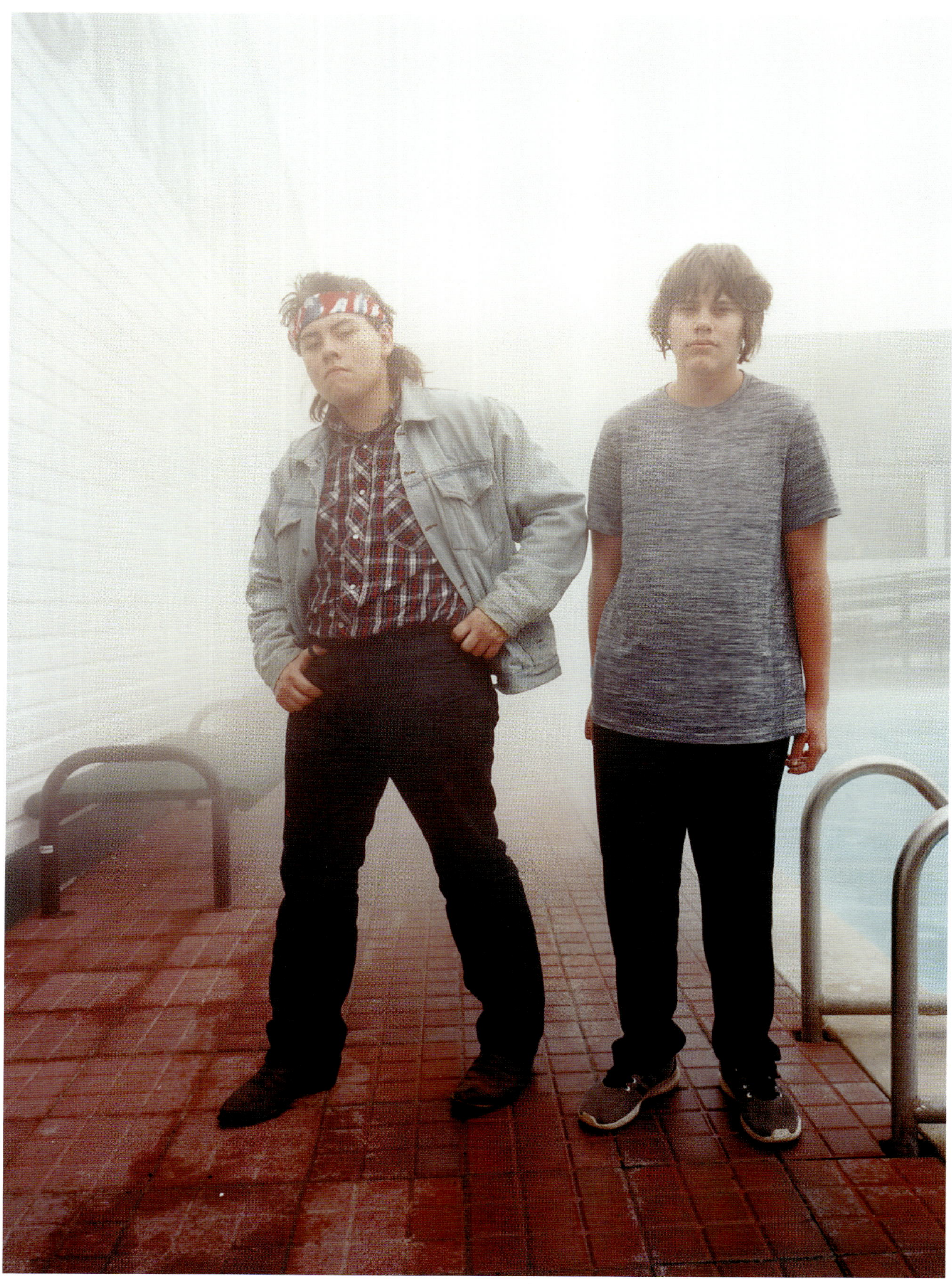

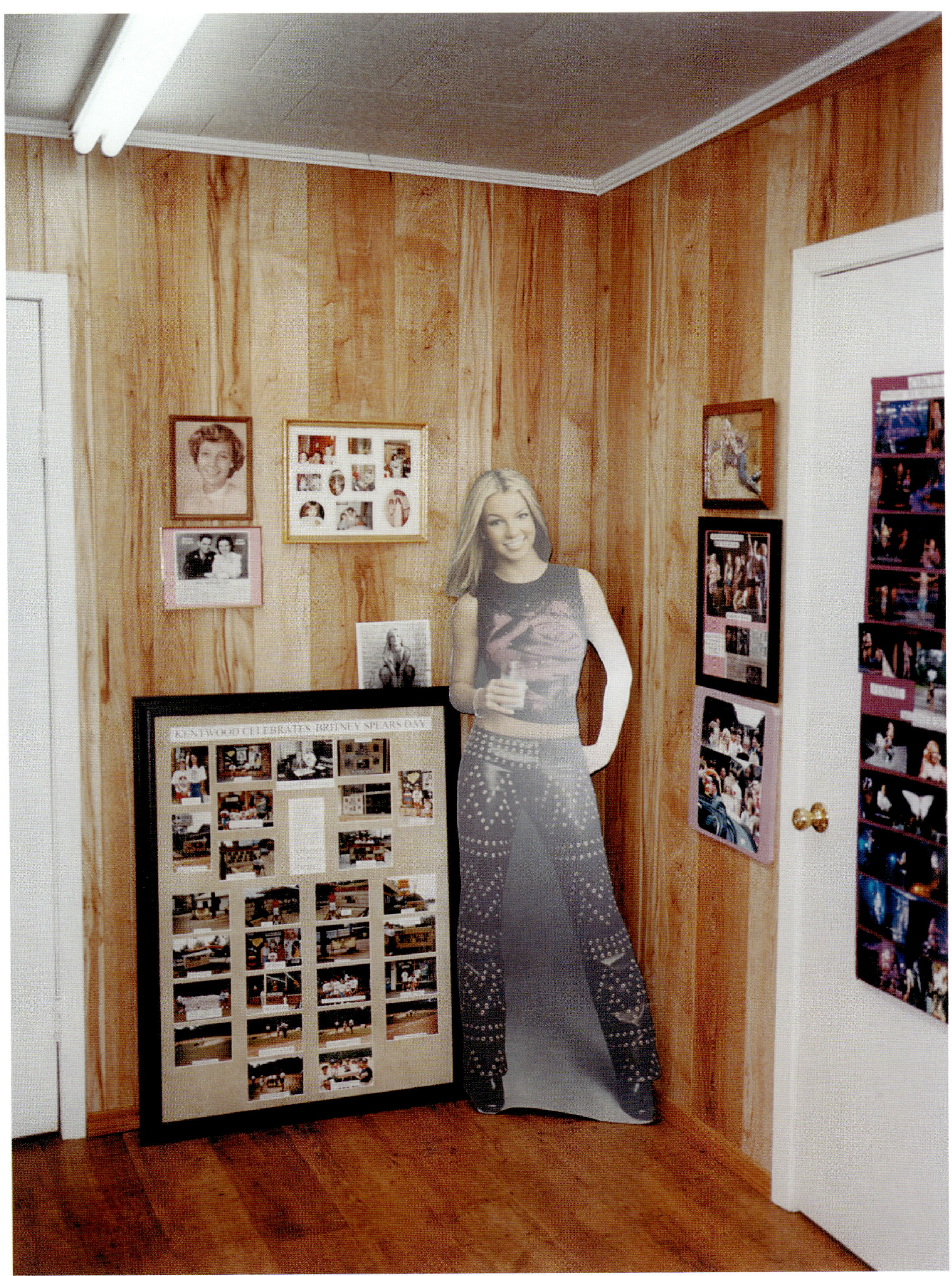
KENTWOOD CELEBRATES BRITNEY SPEARS DAY

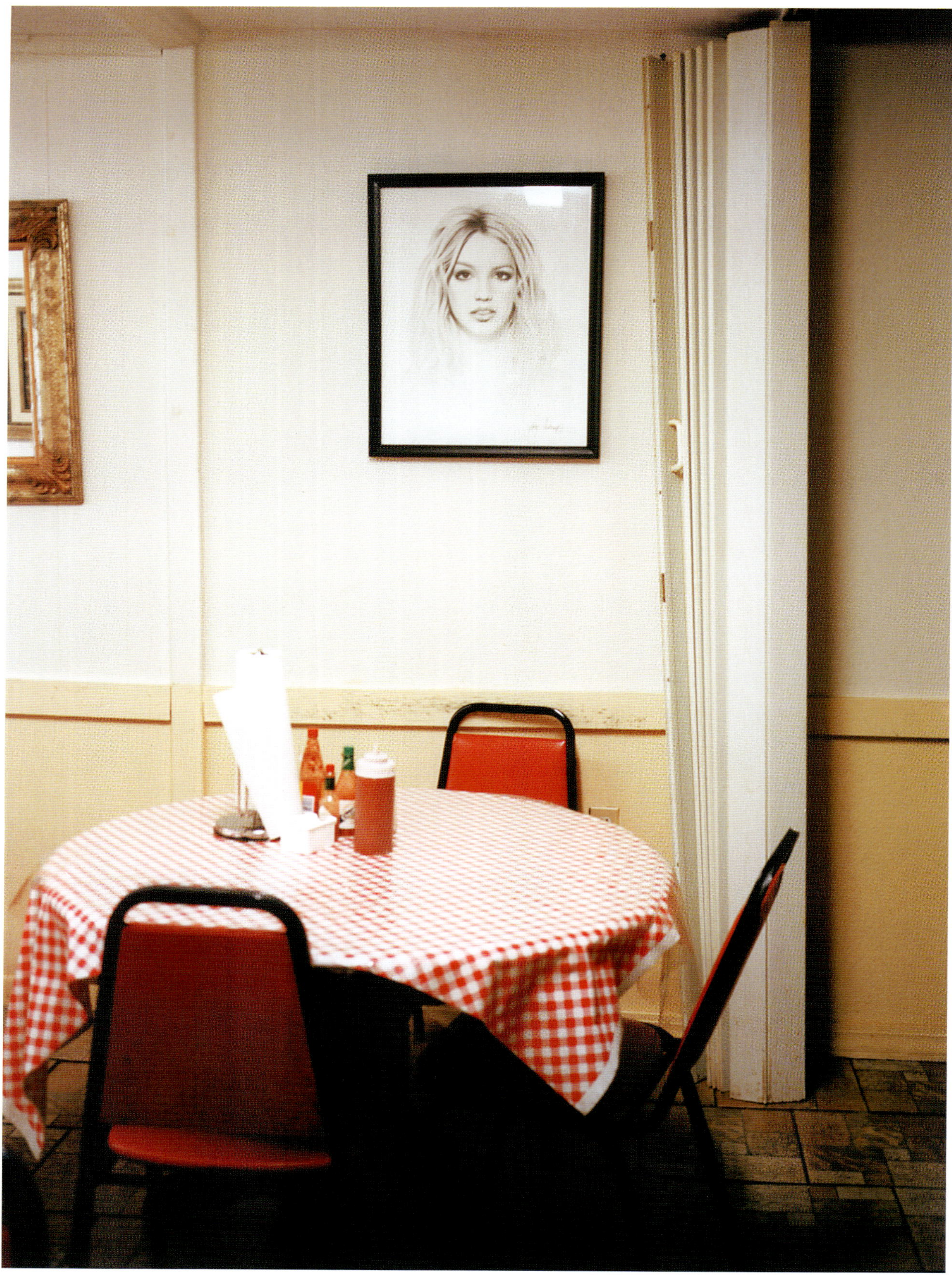

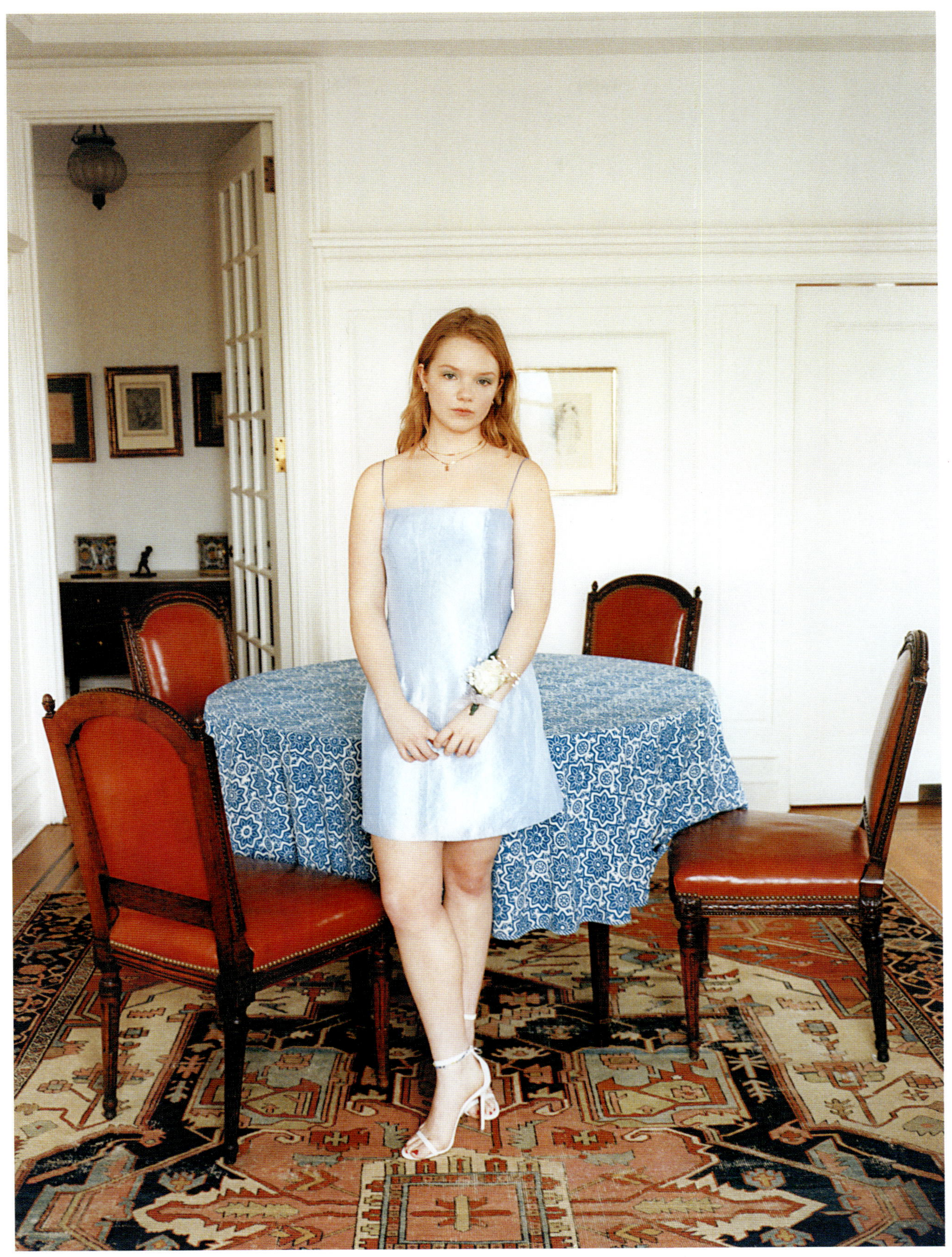

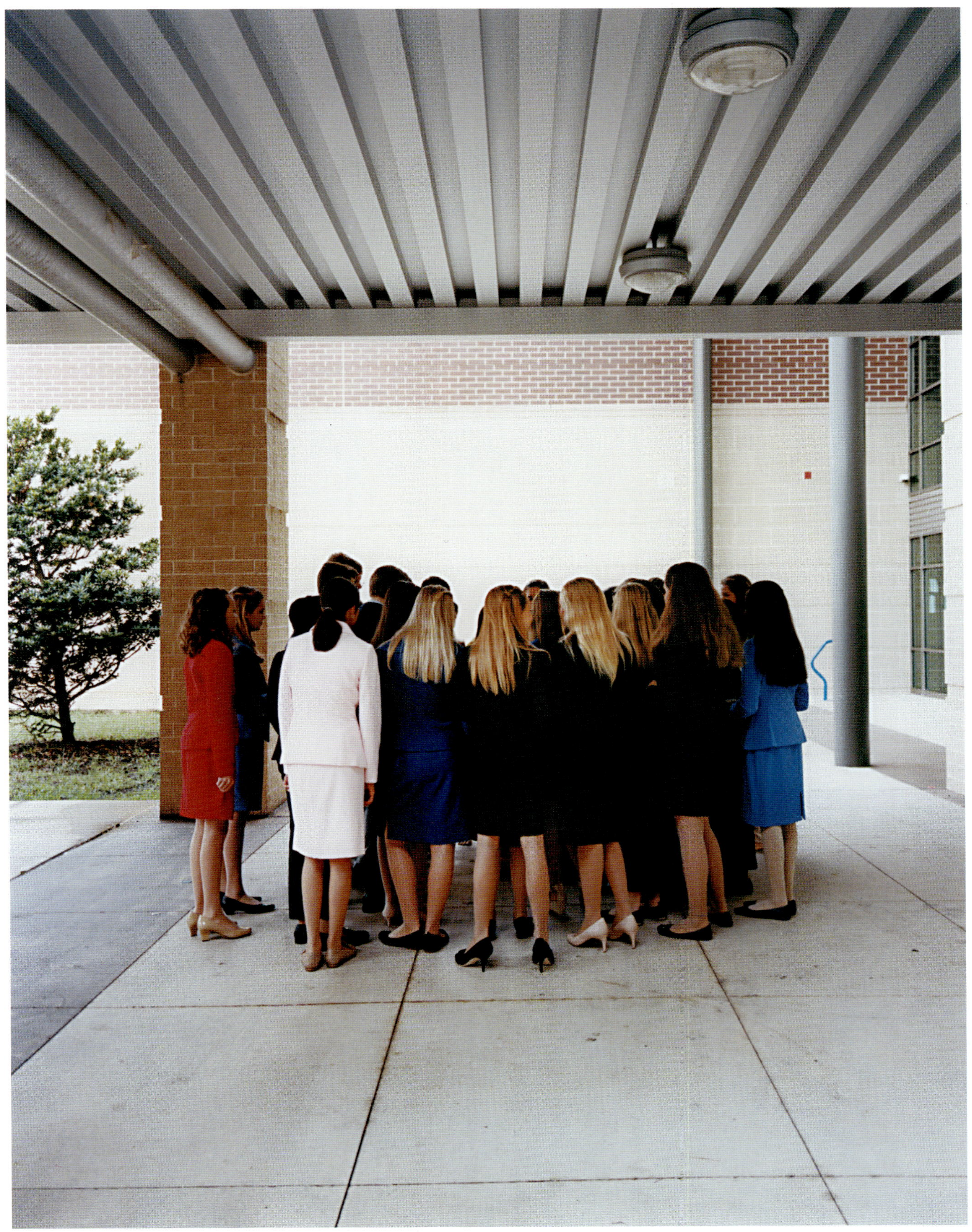

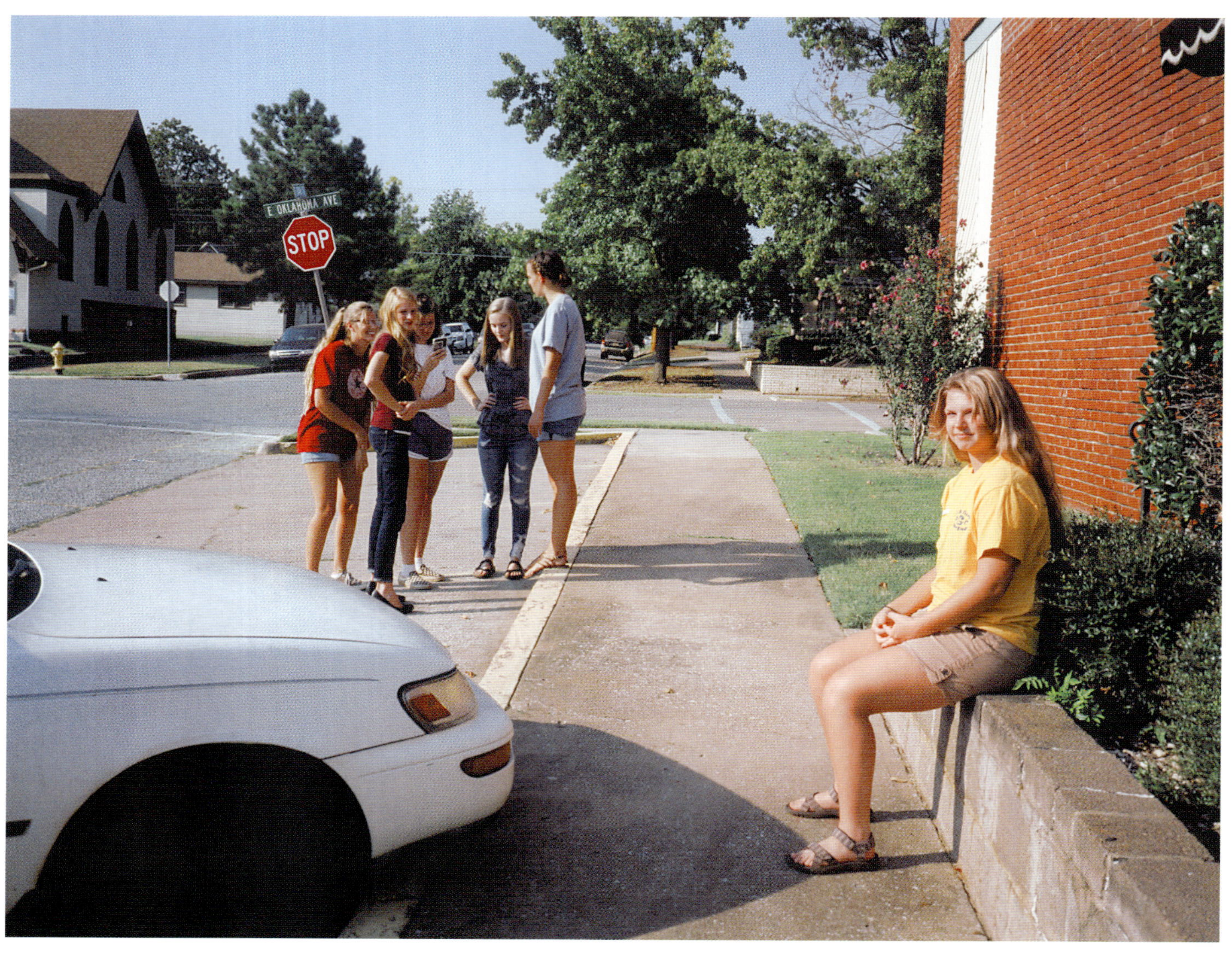
E OKLAHOMA AVE
STOP

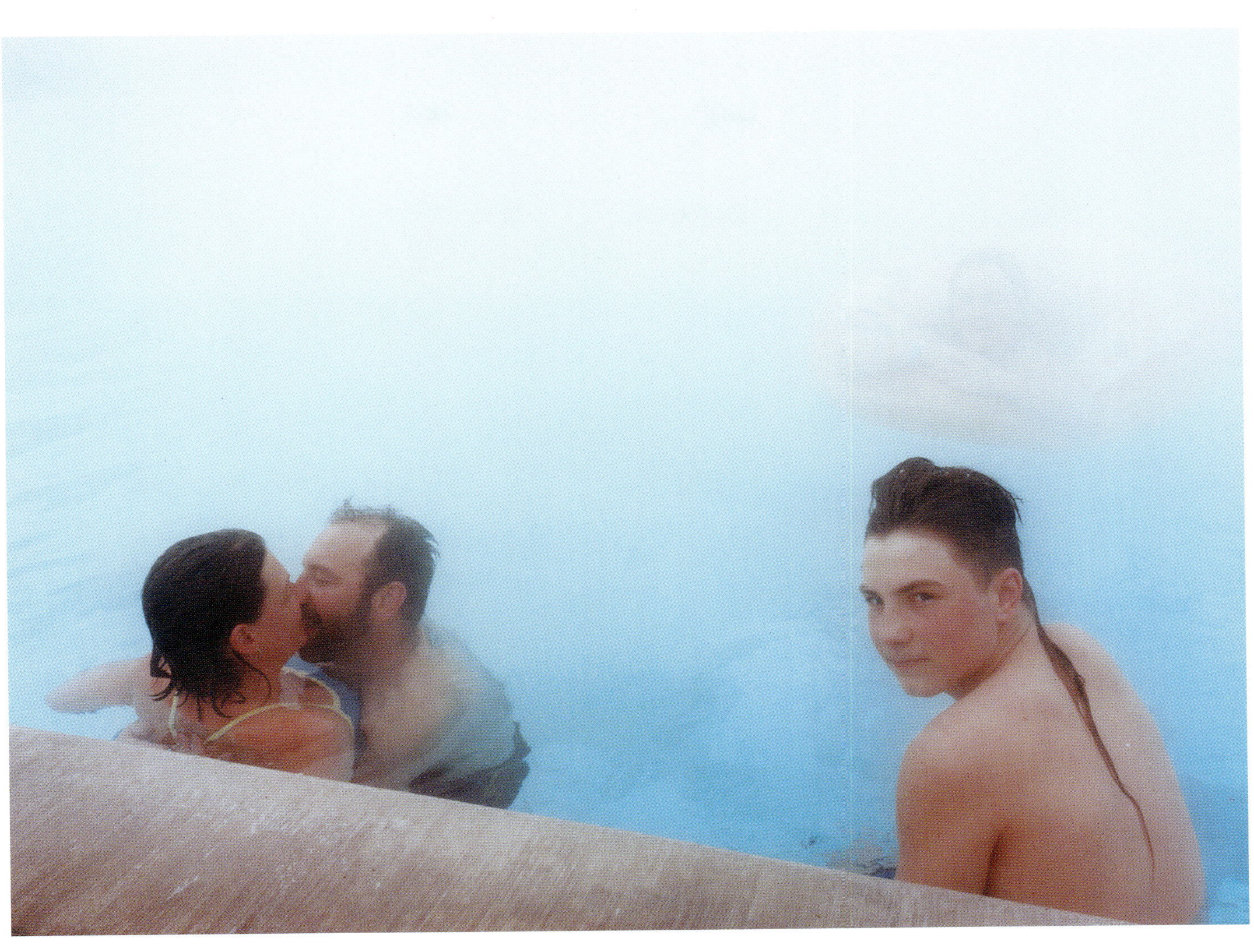

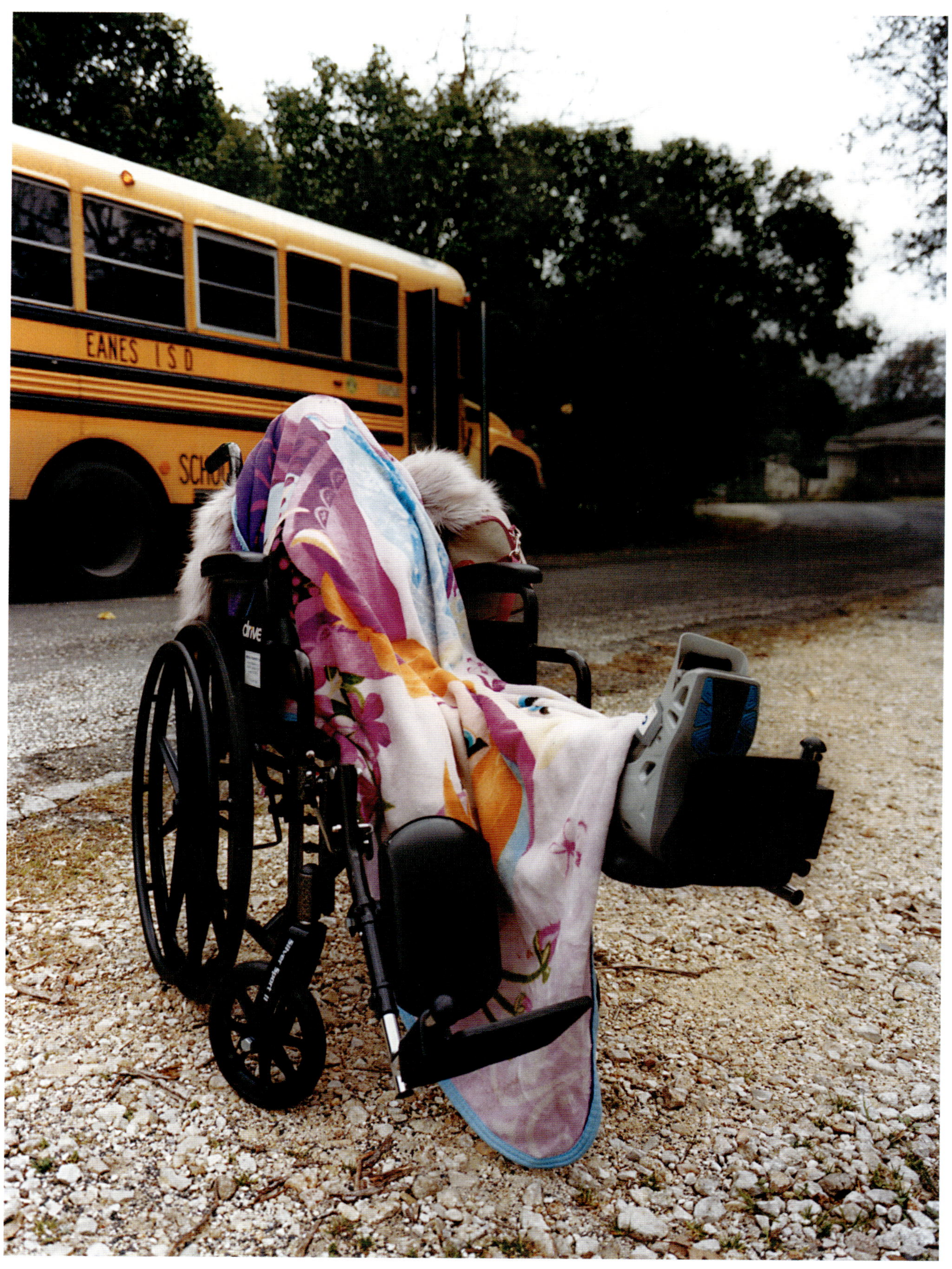
EANES I S D
drive

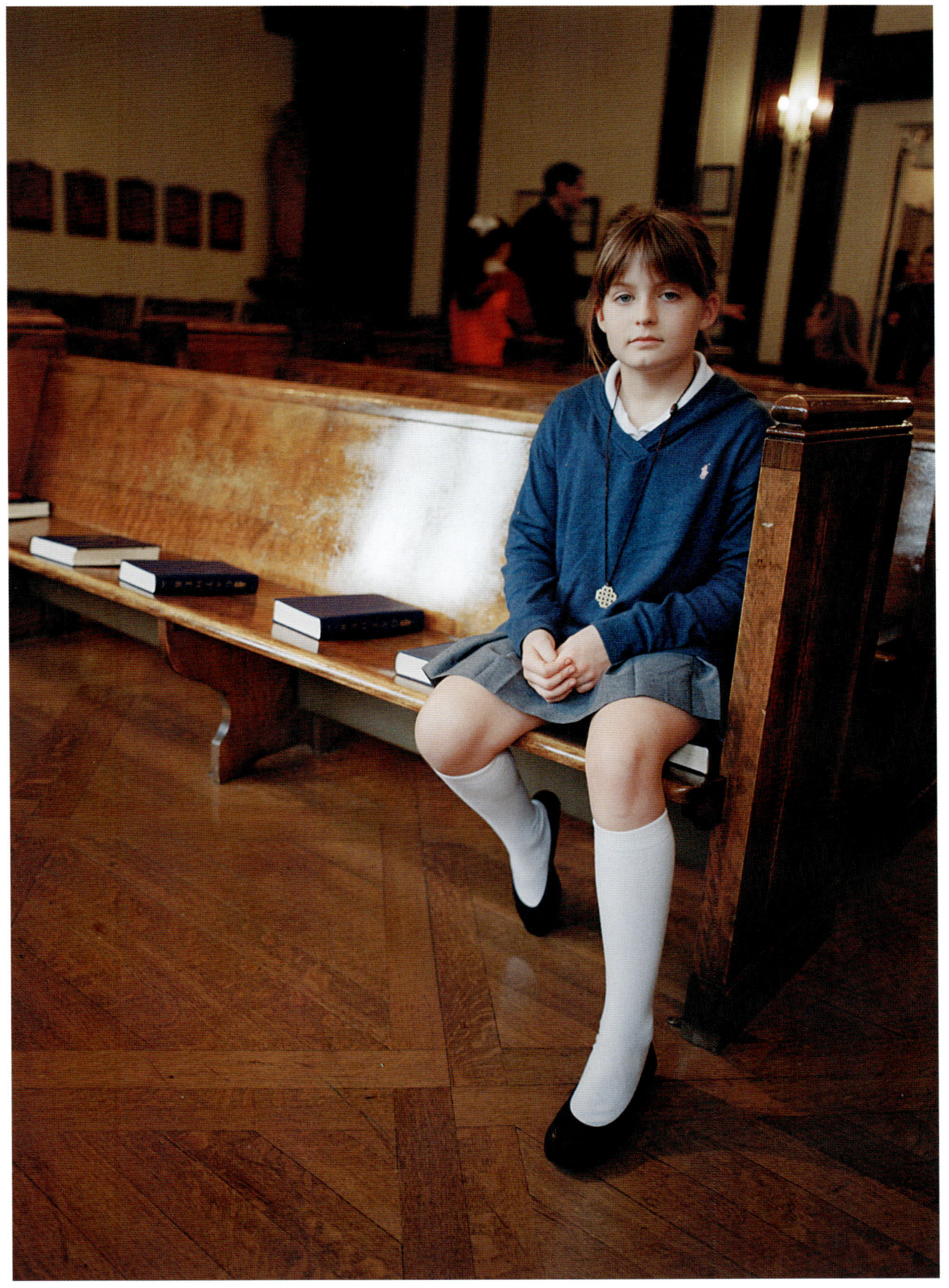

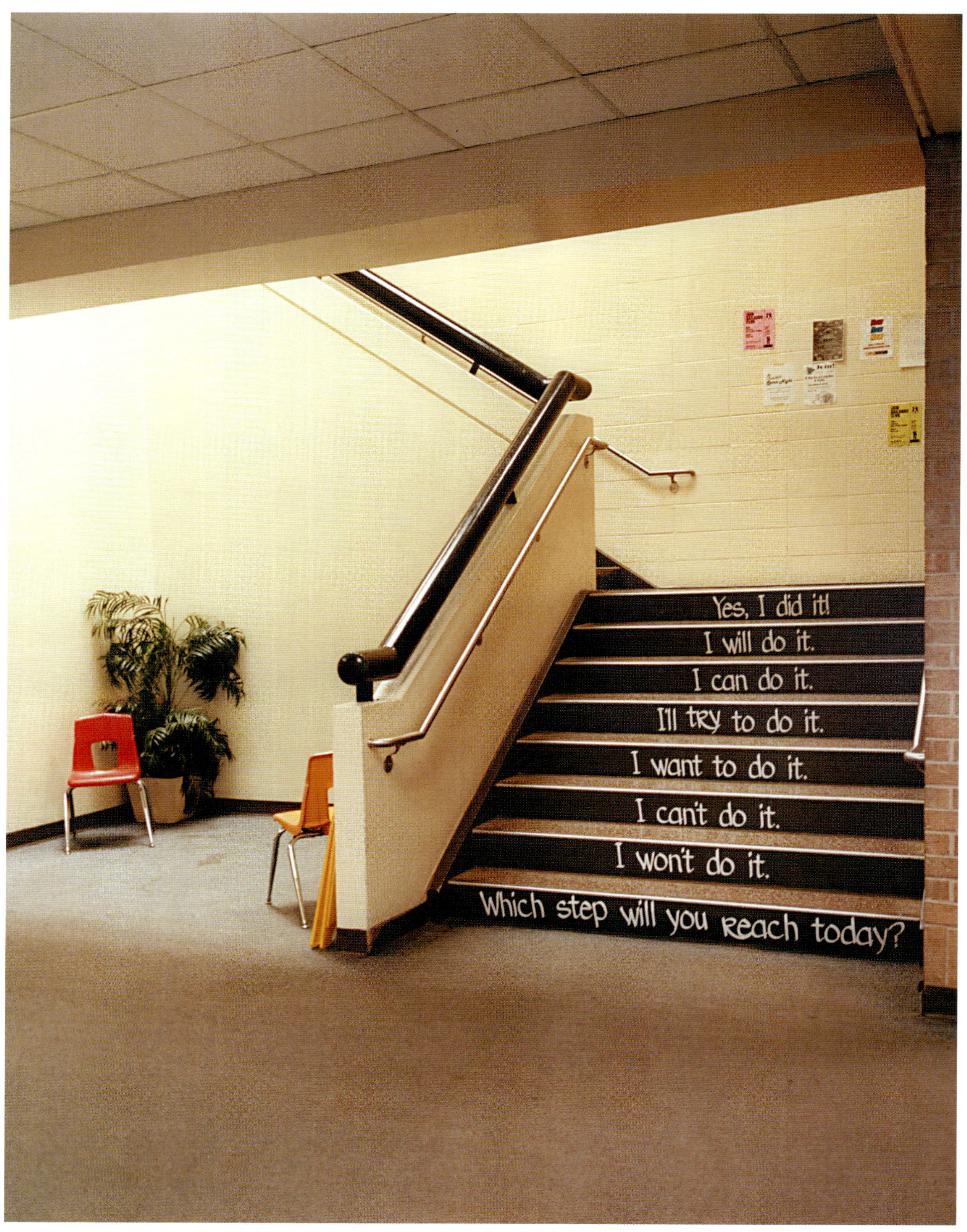
Yes, I did it!
I will do it.
I can do it.
I'll try to do it.
I want to do it.
I can't do it.
I won't do it.
Which step will you reach today?

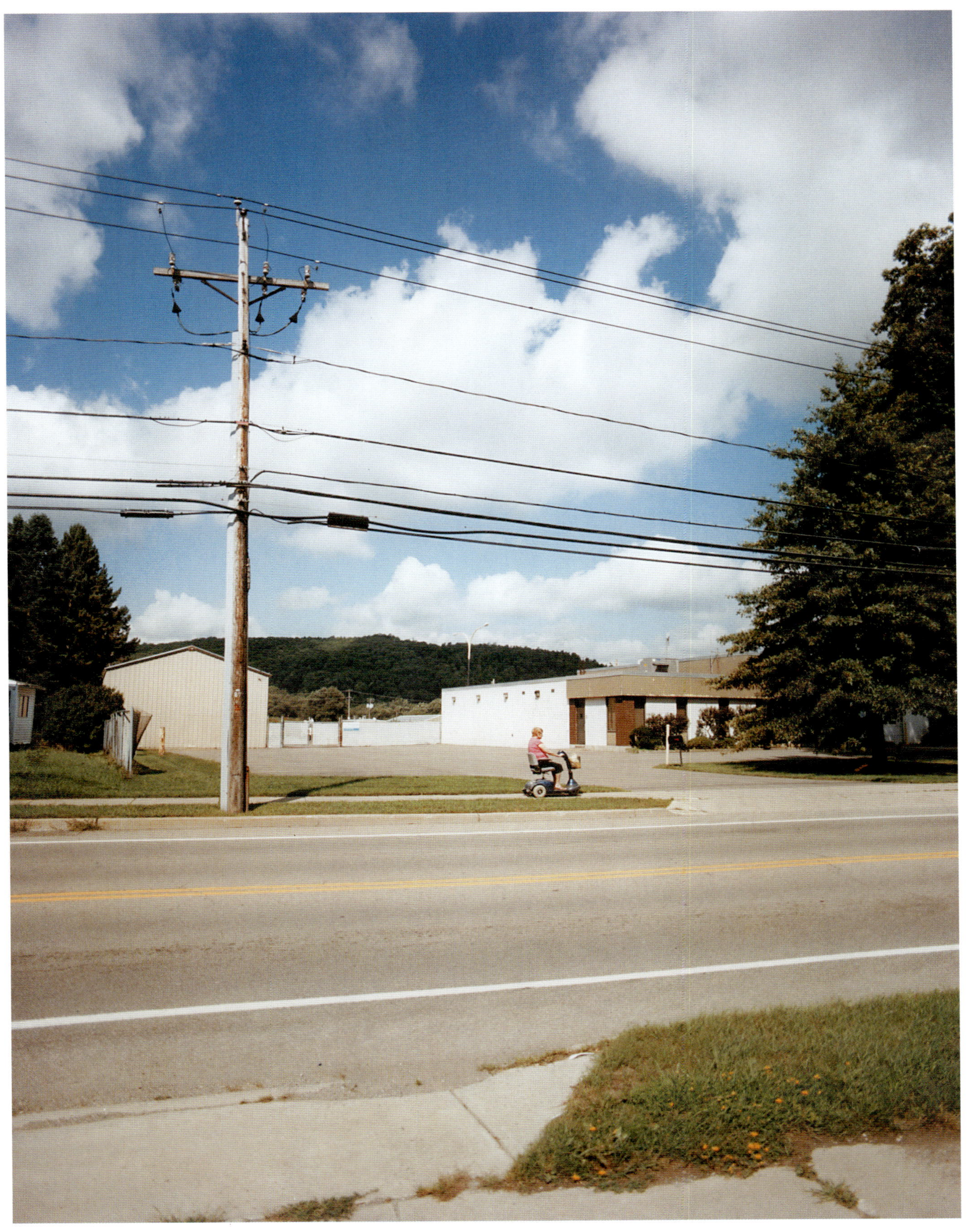

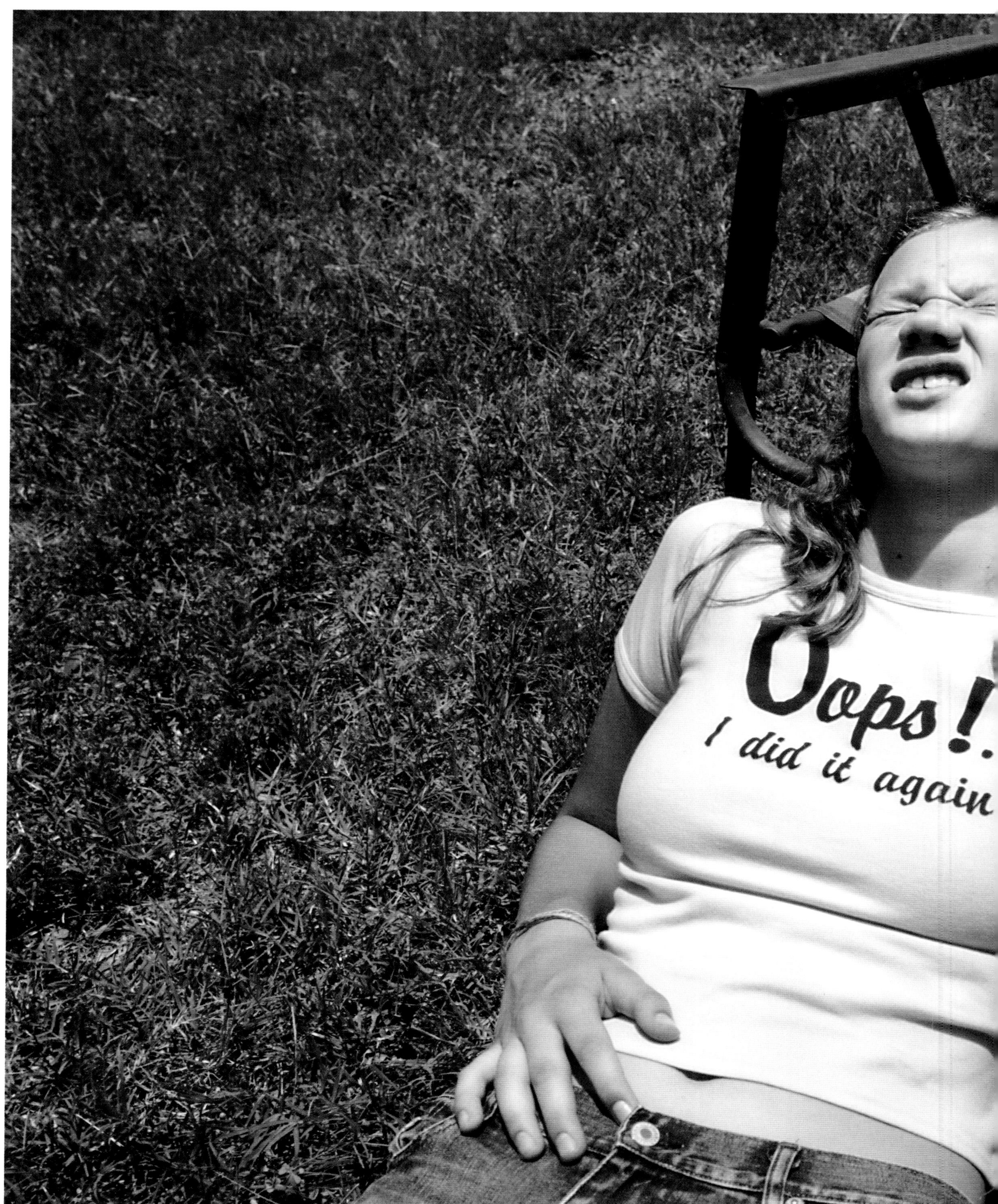
Oops!
I did it again

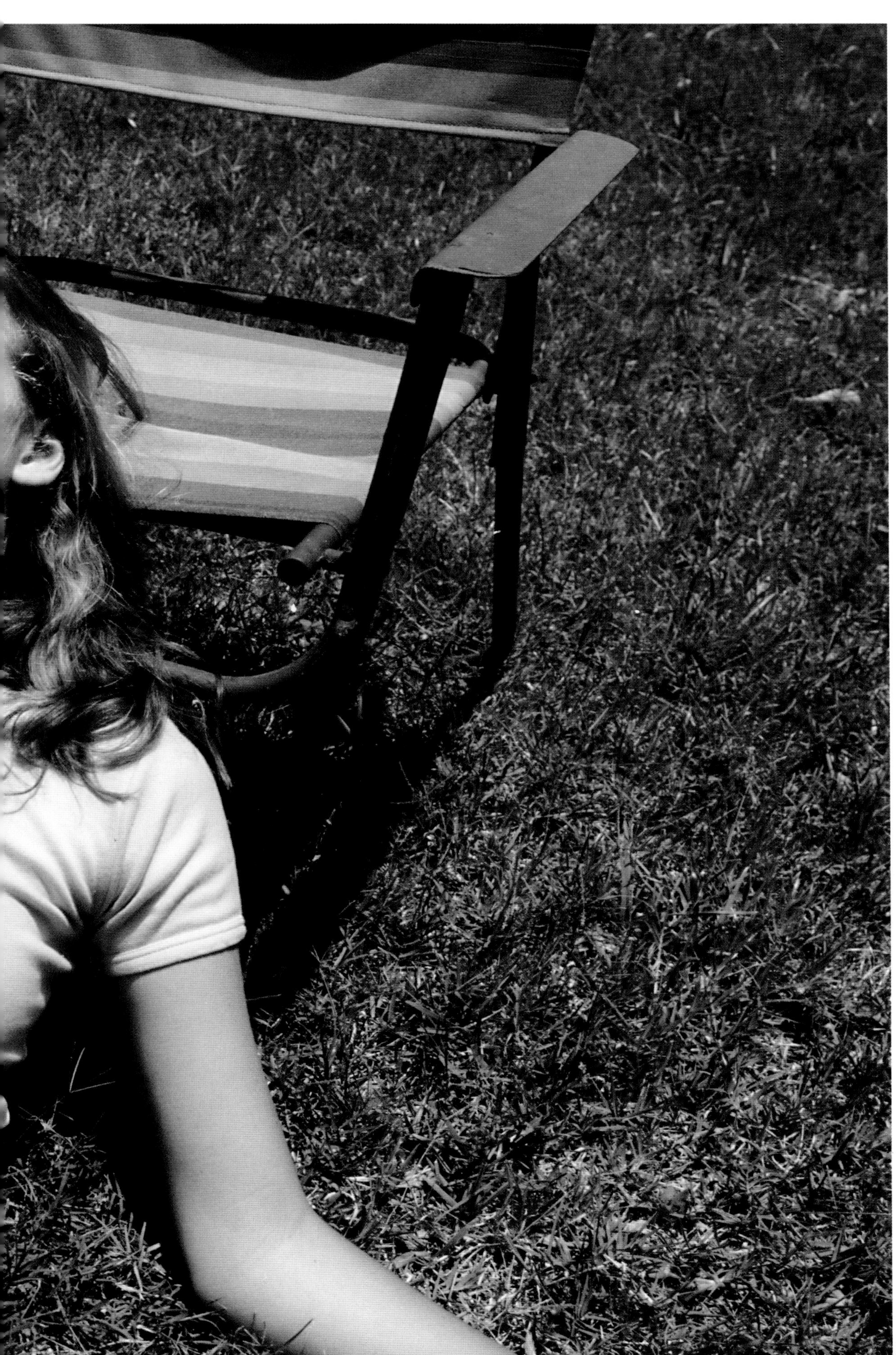

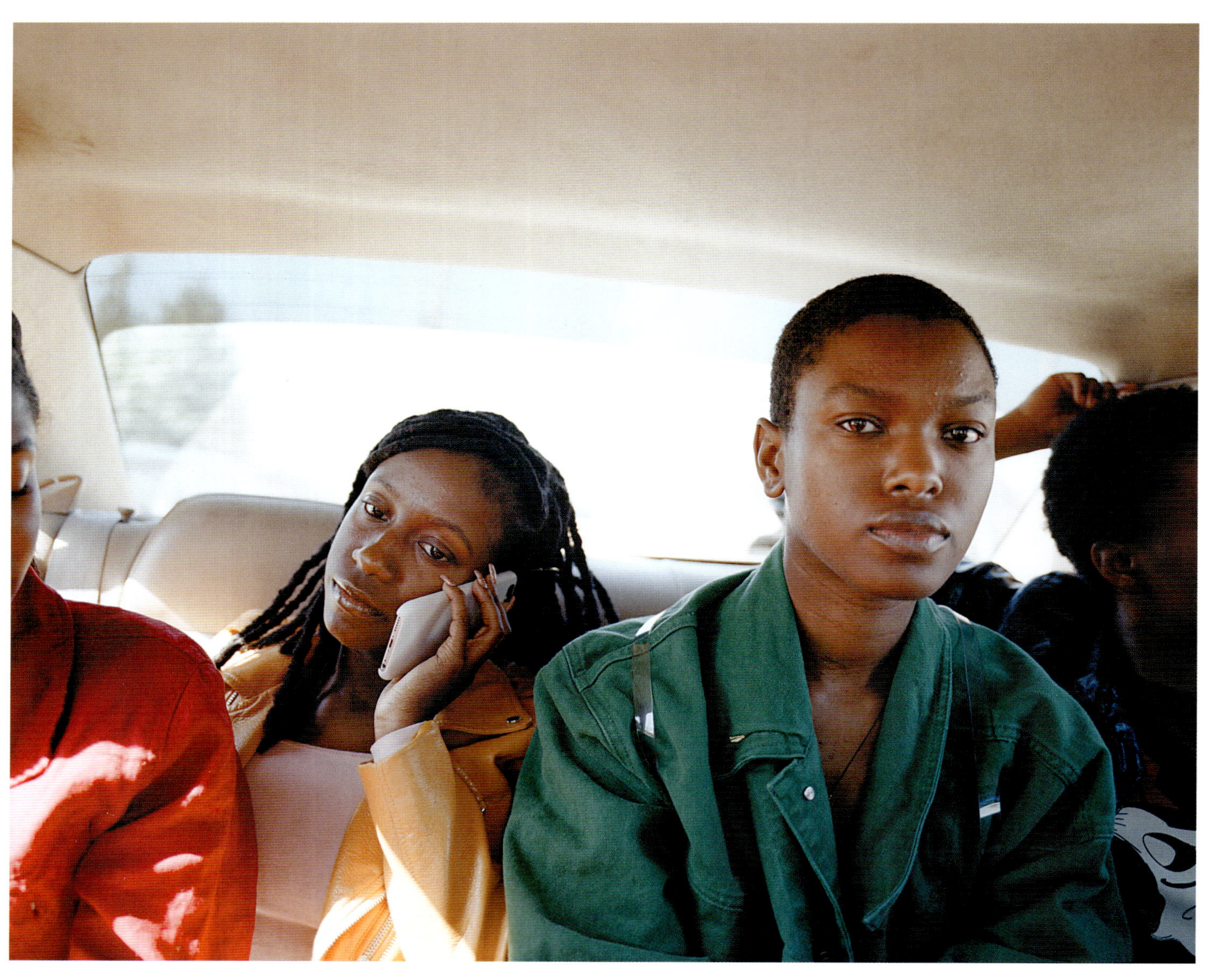

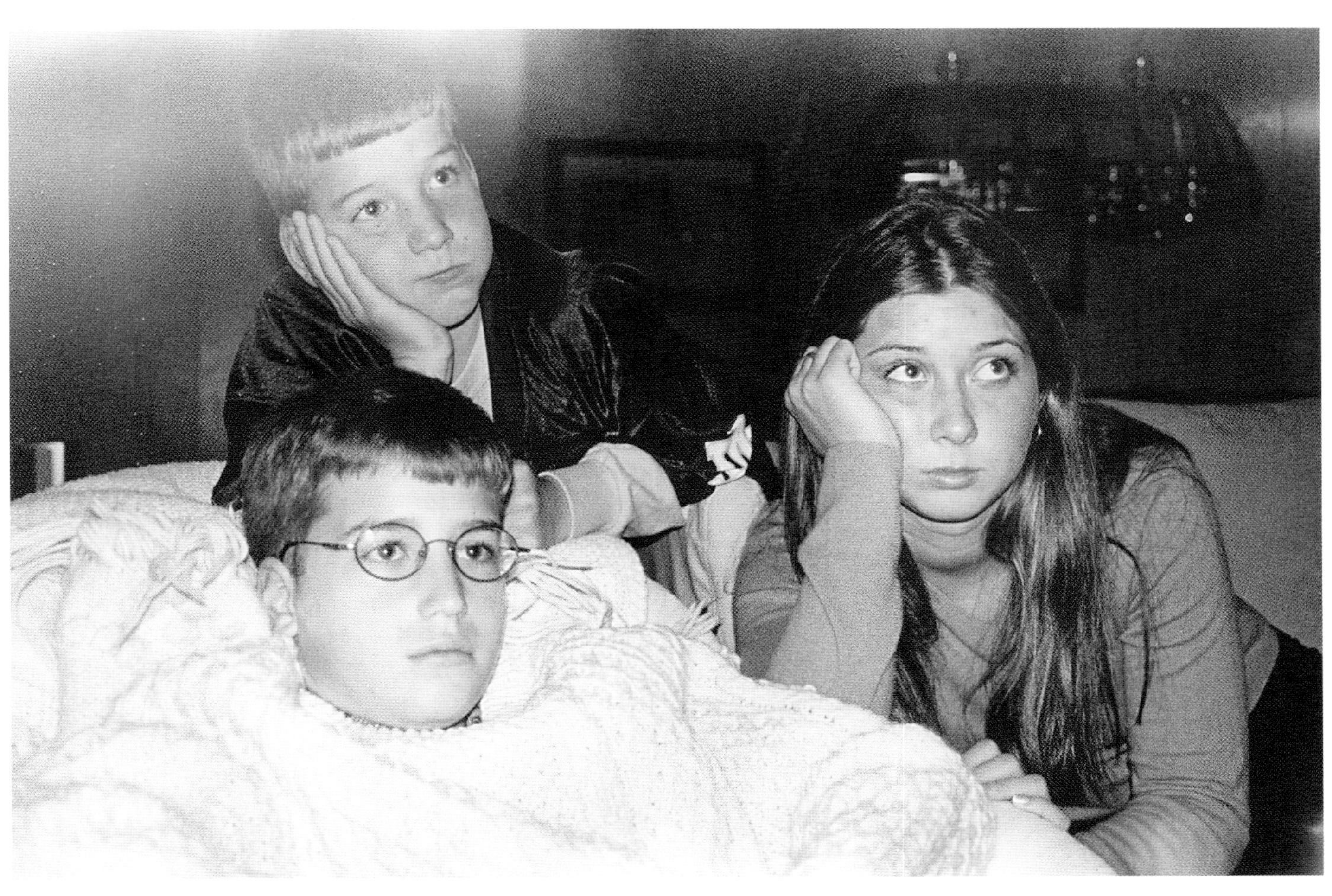

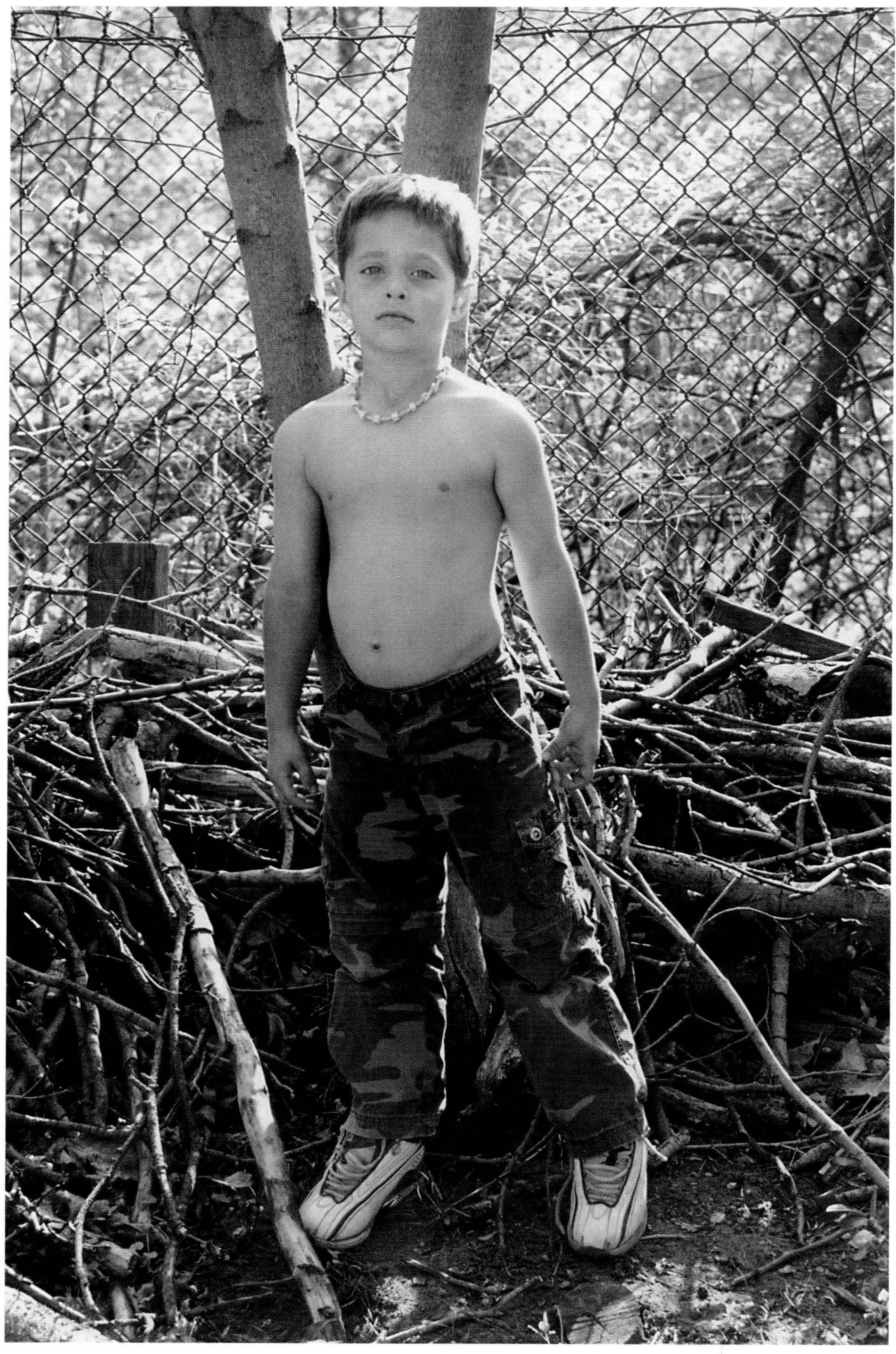

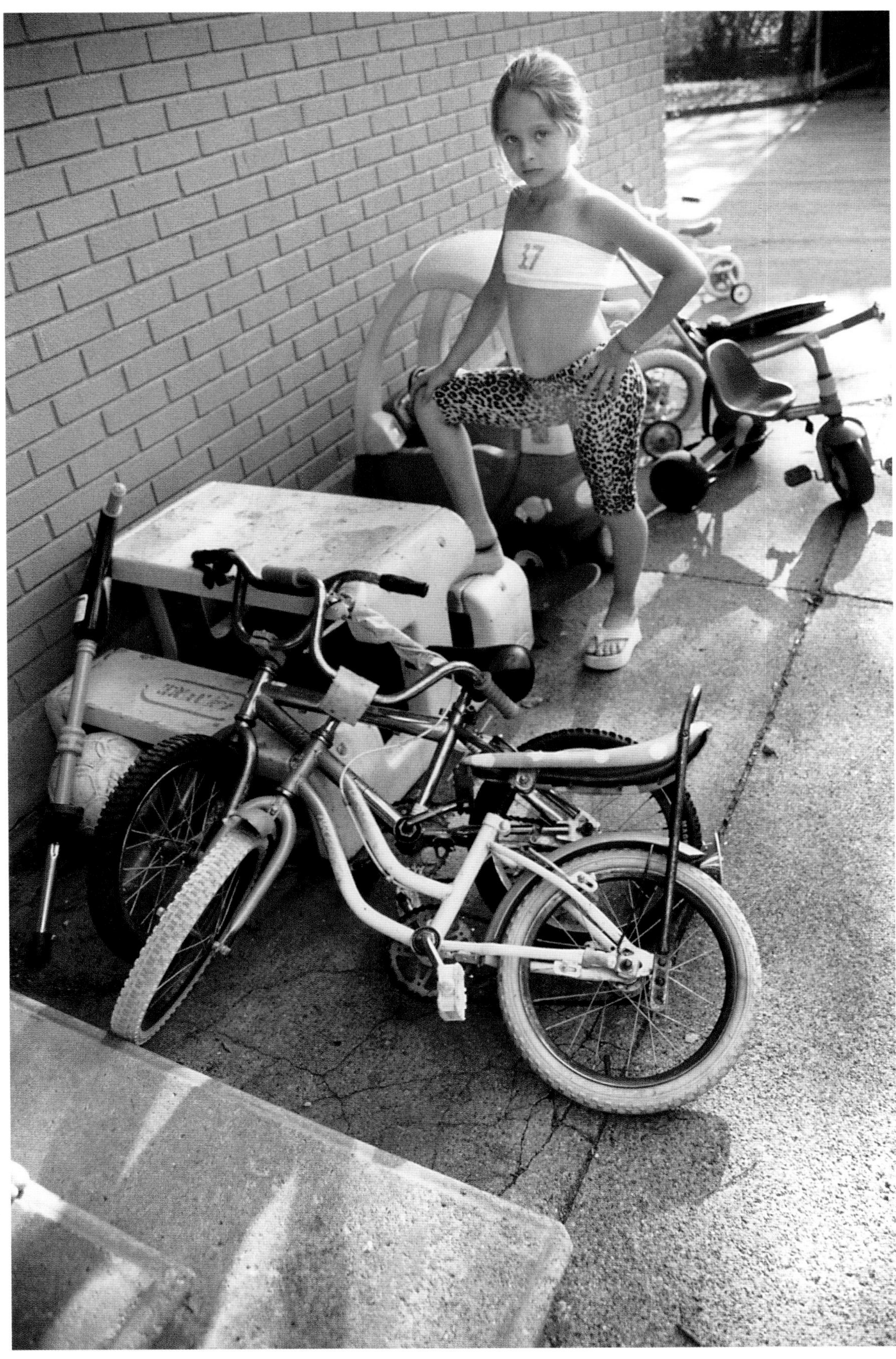
17

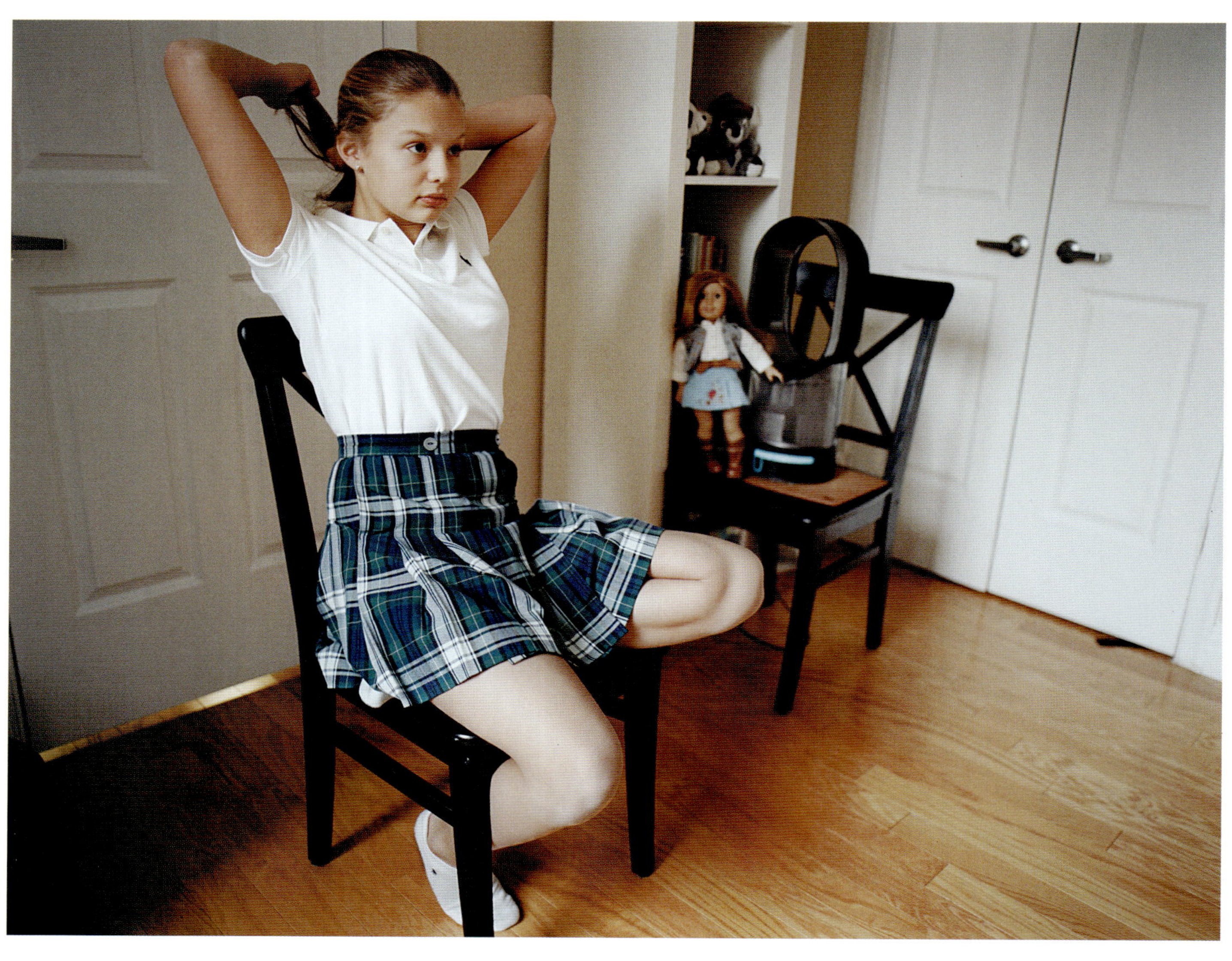

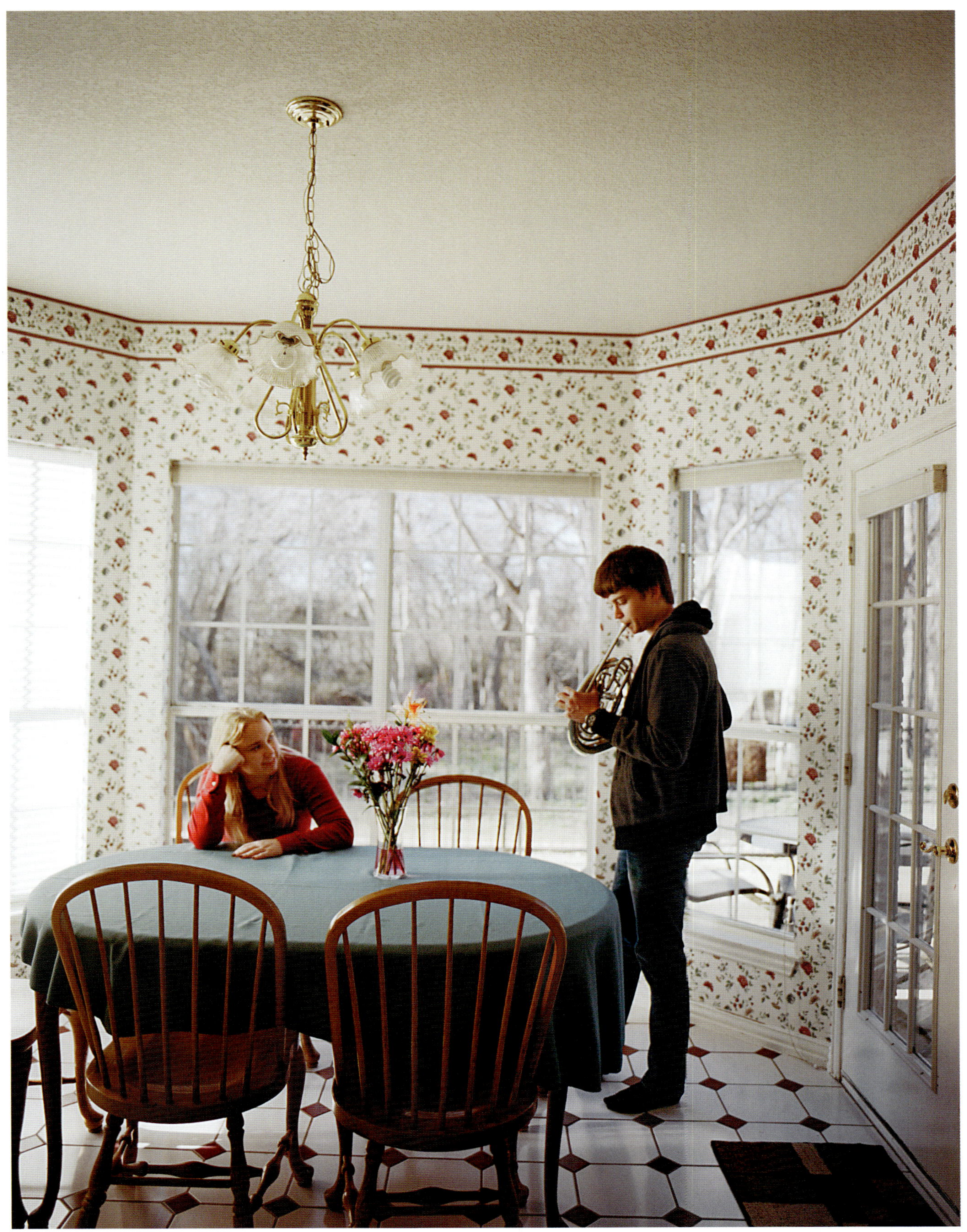

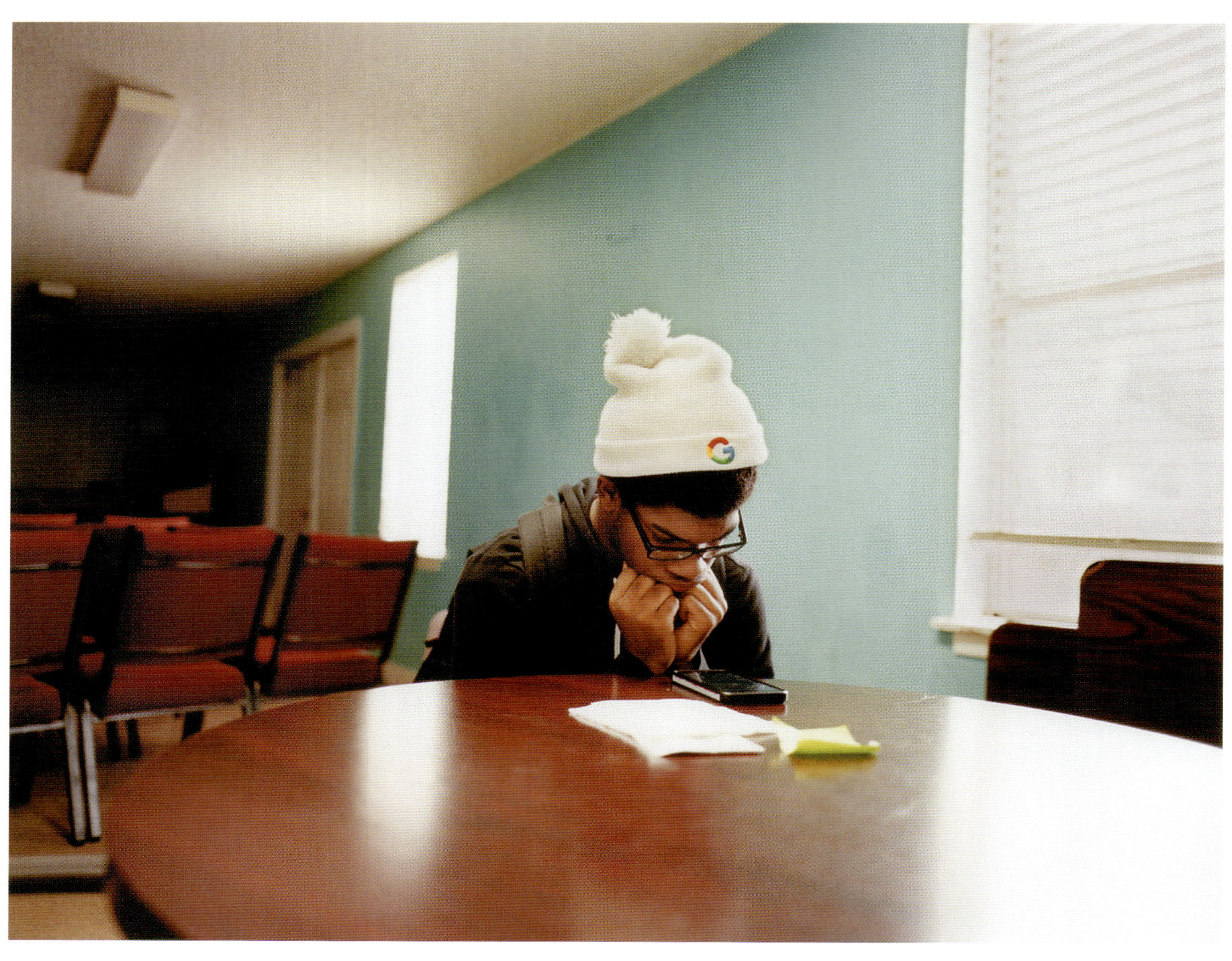

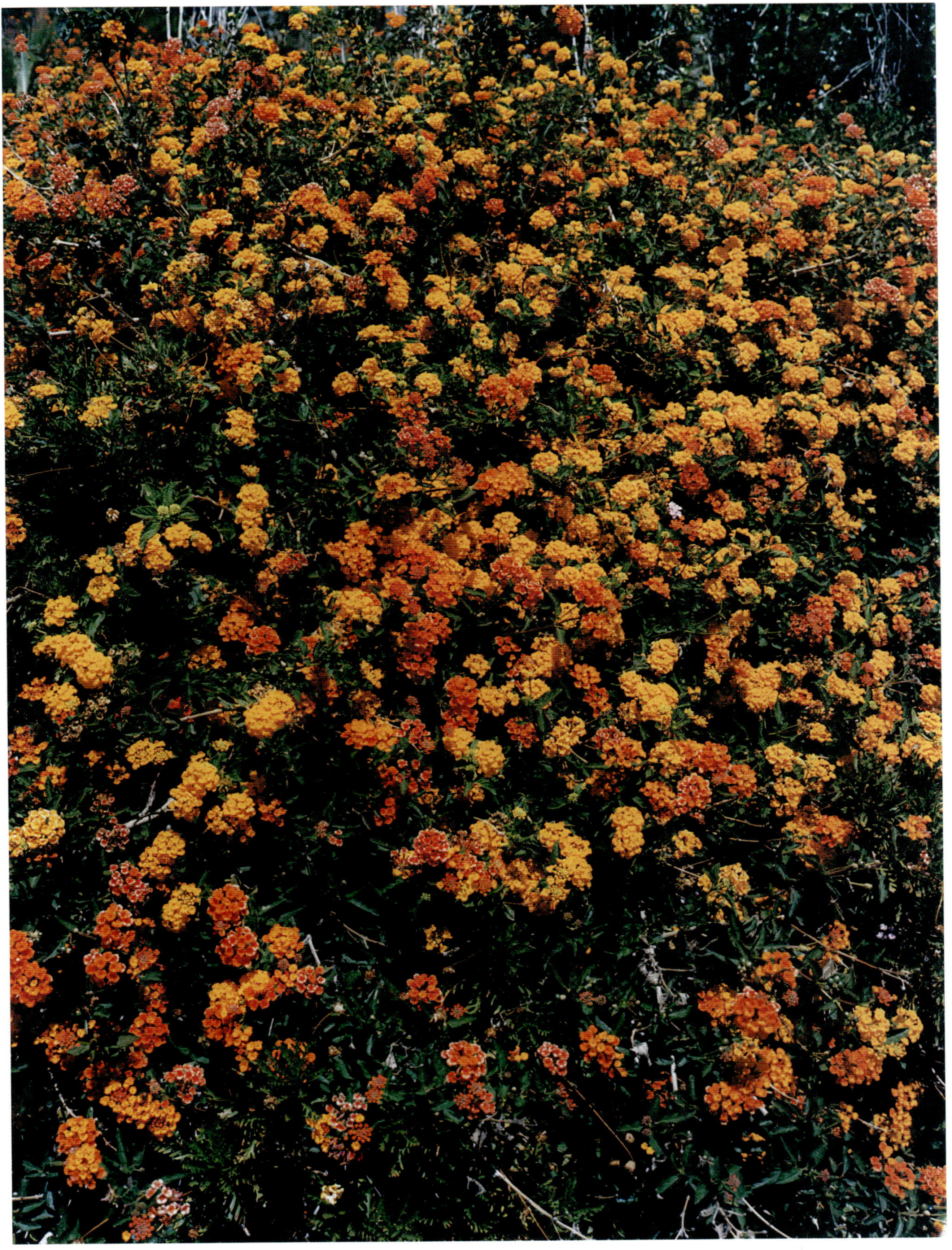

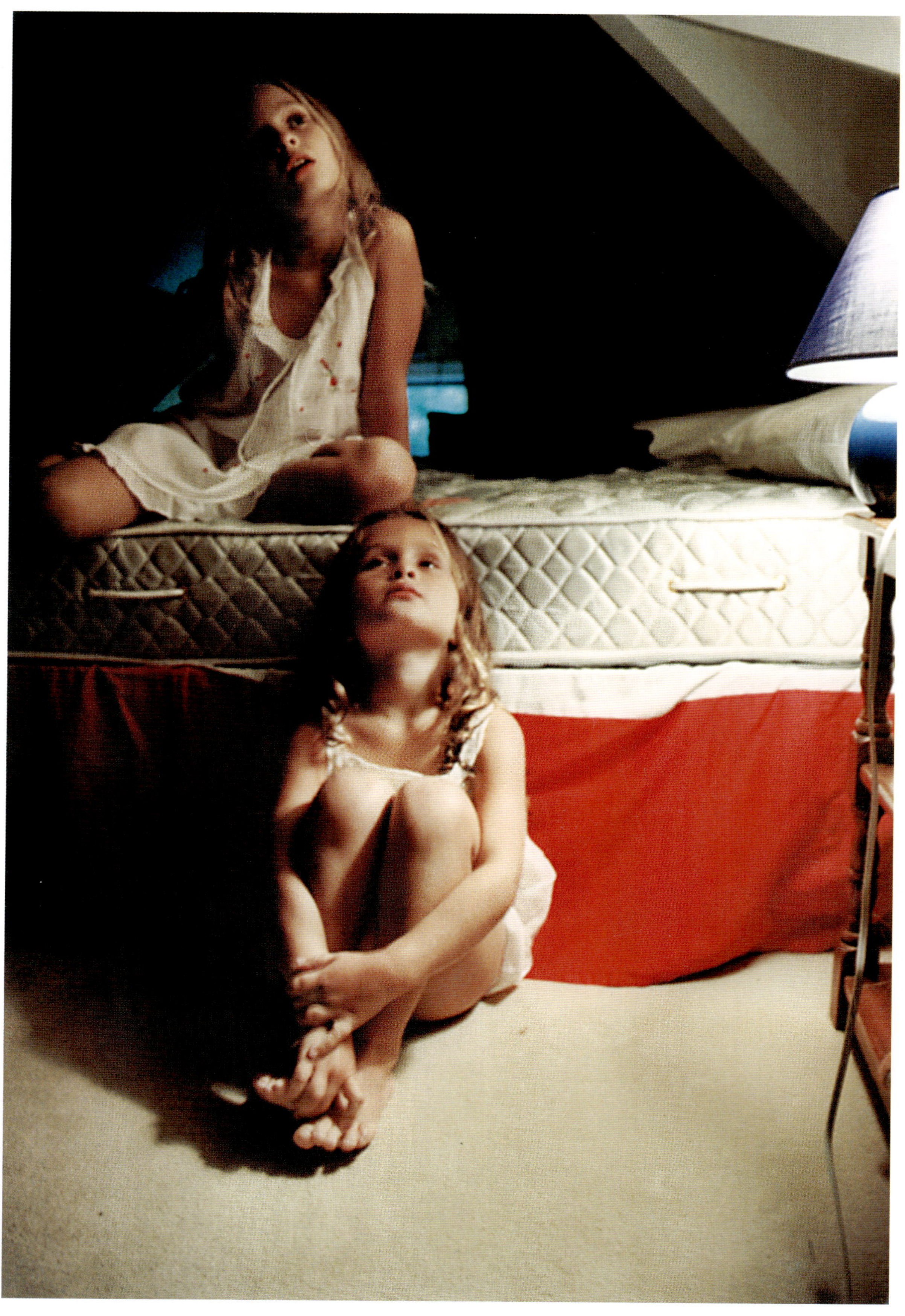

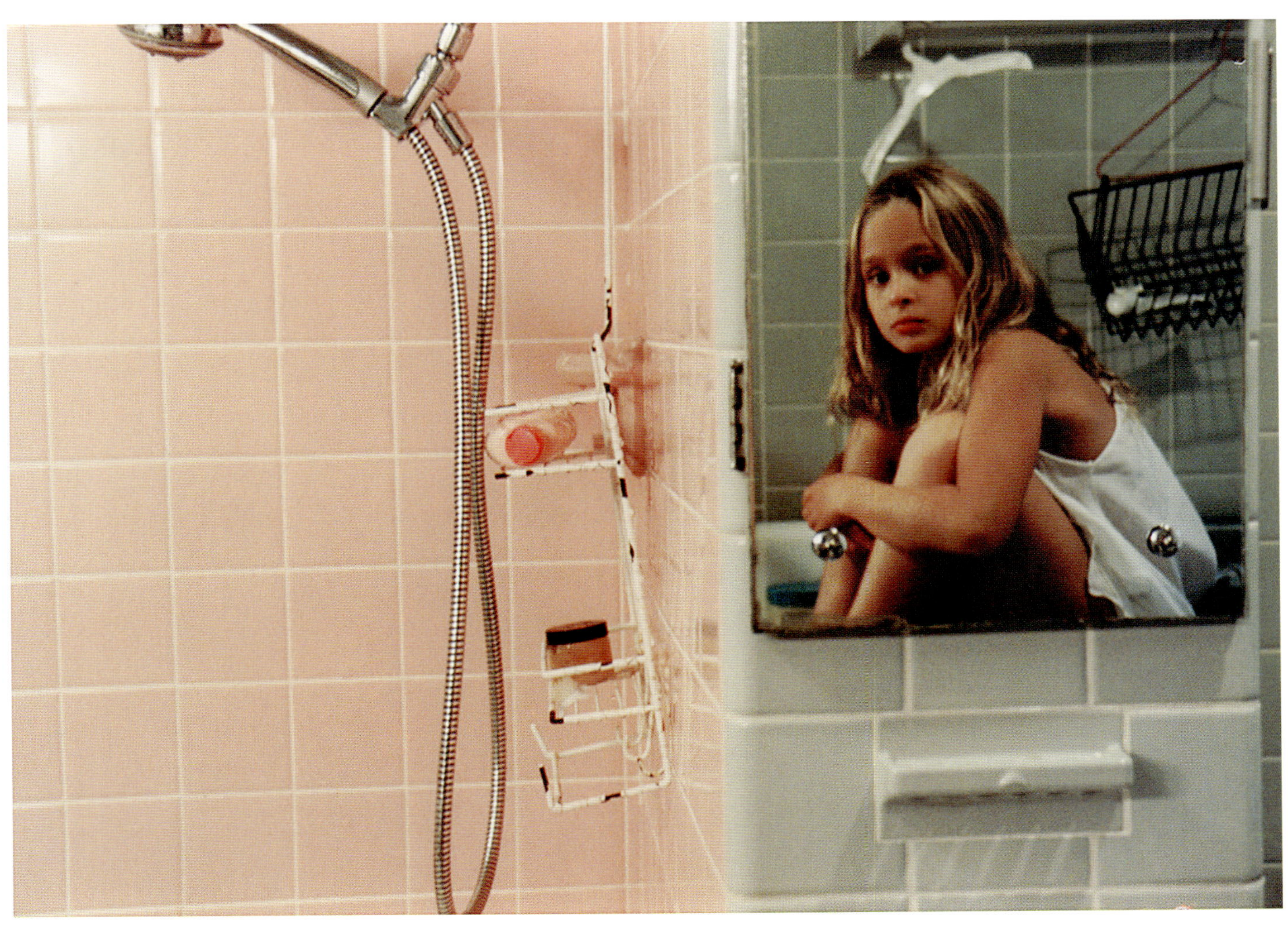

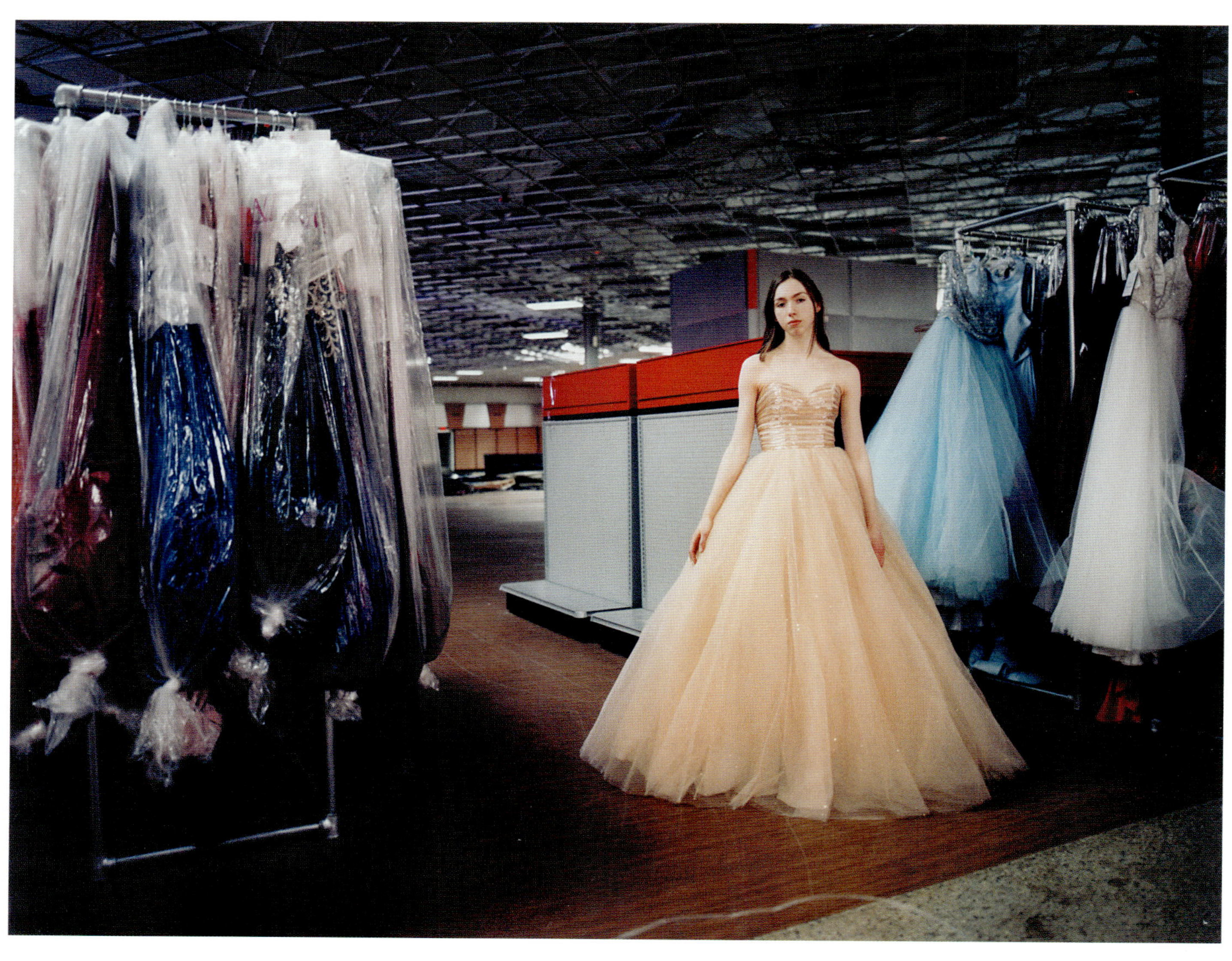

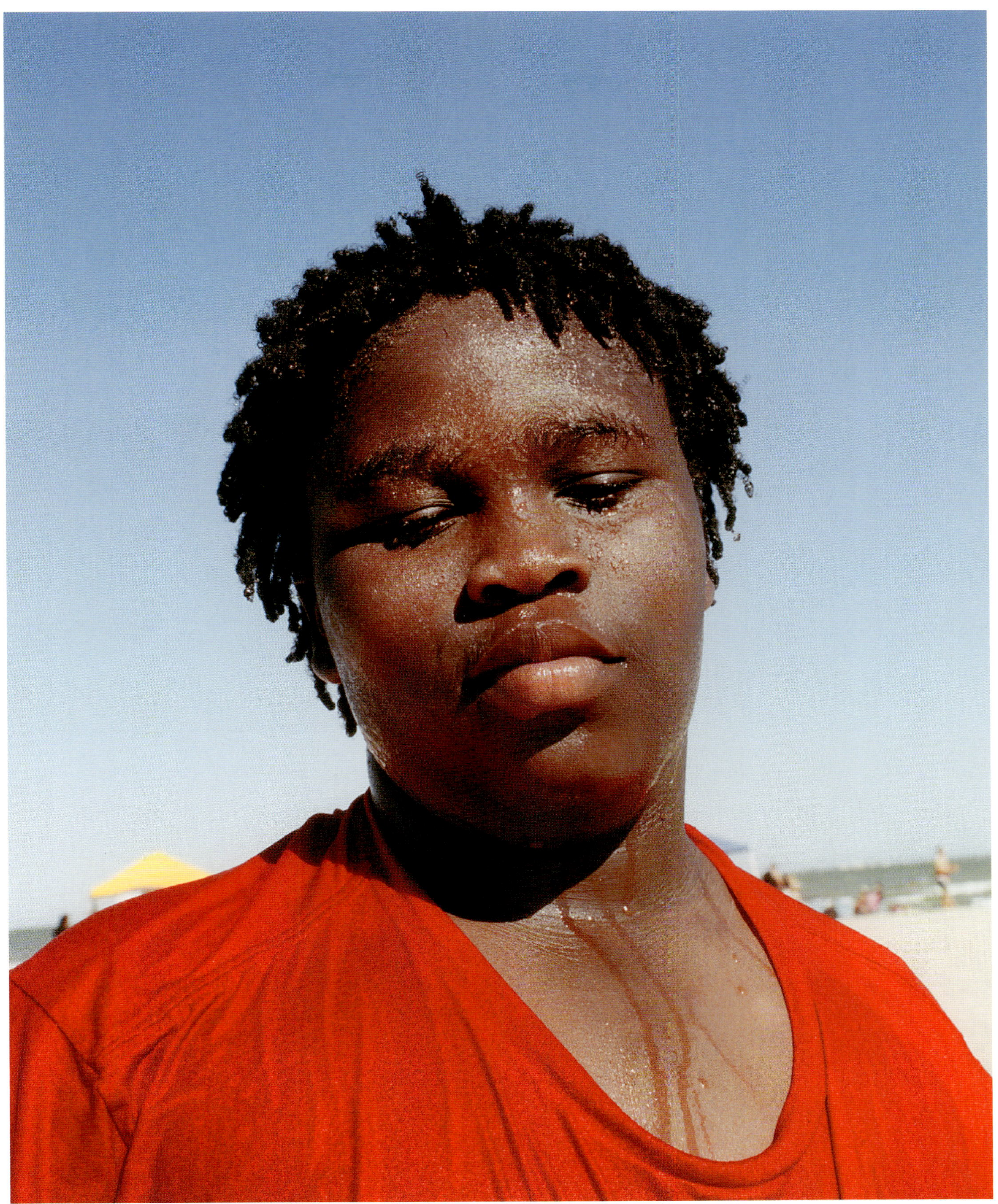

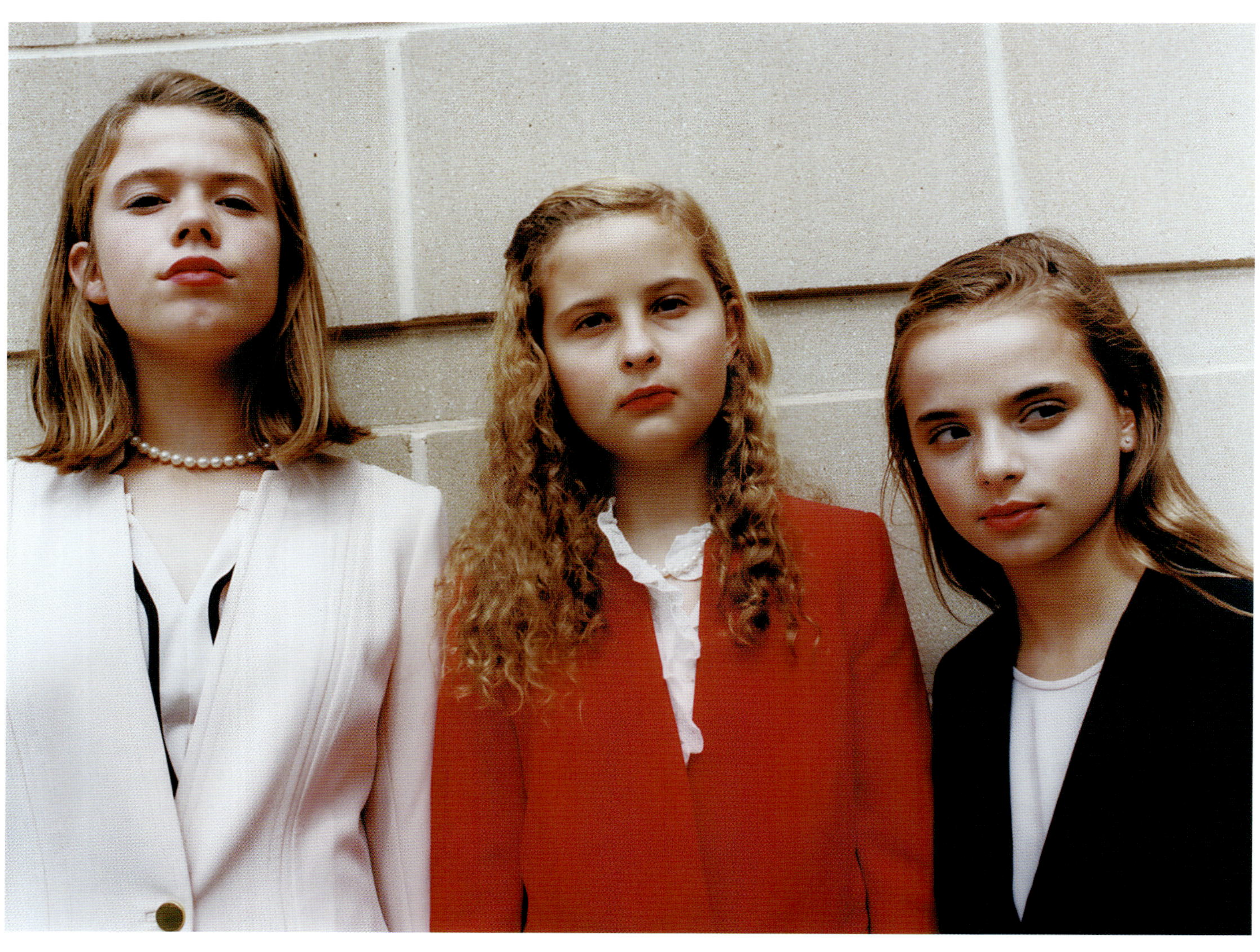

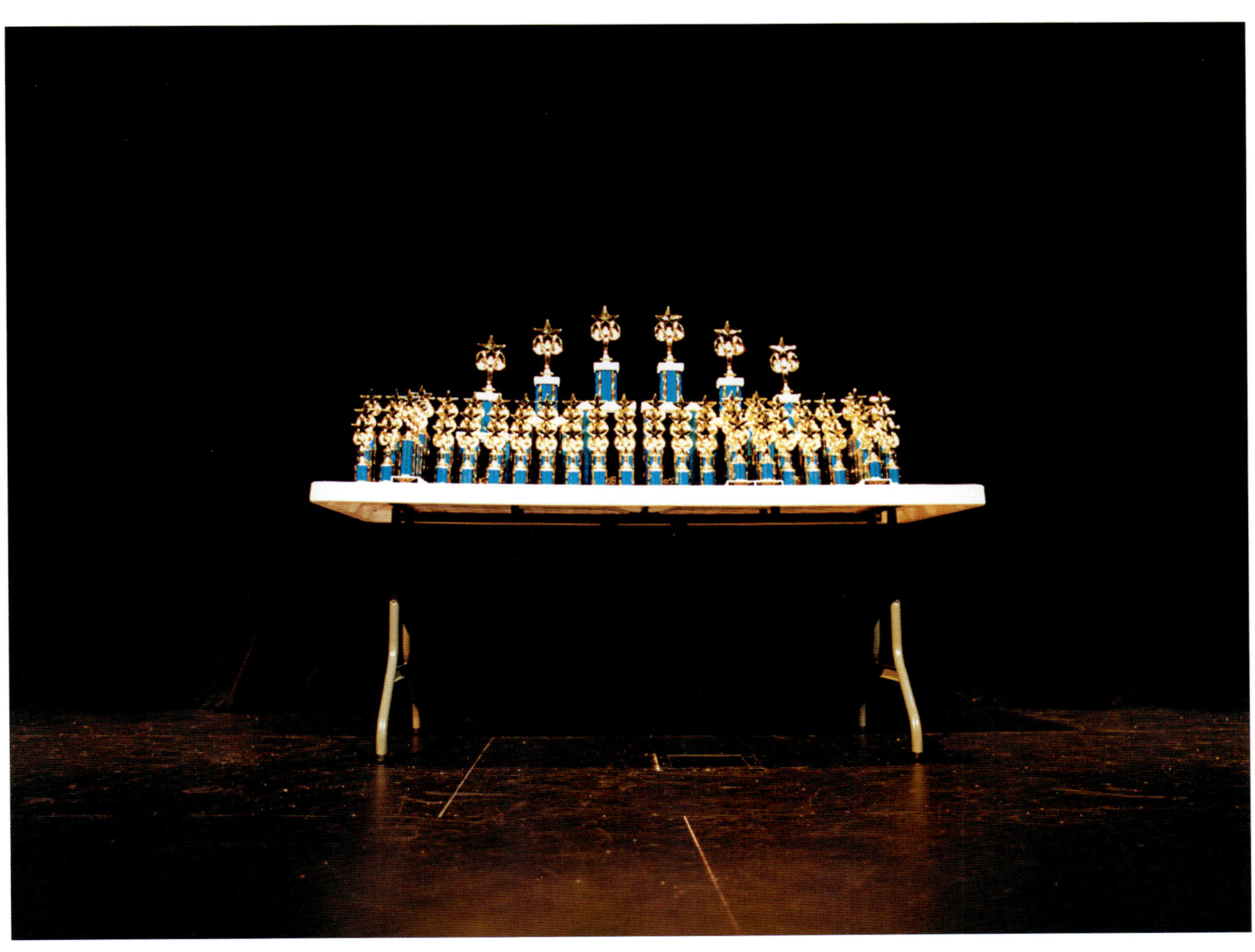

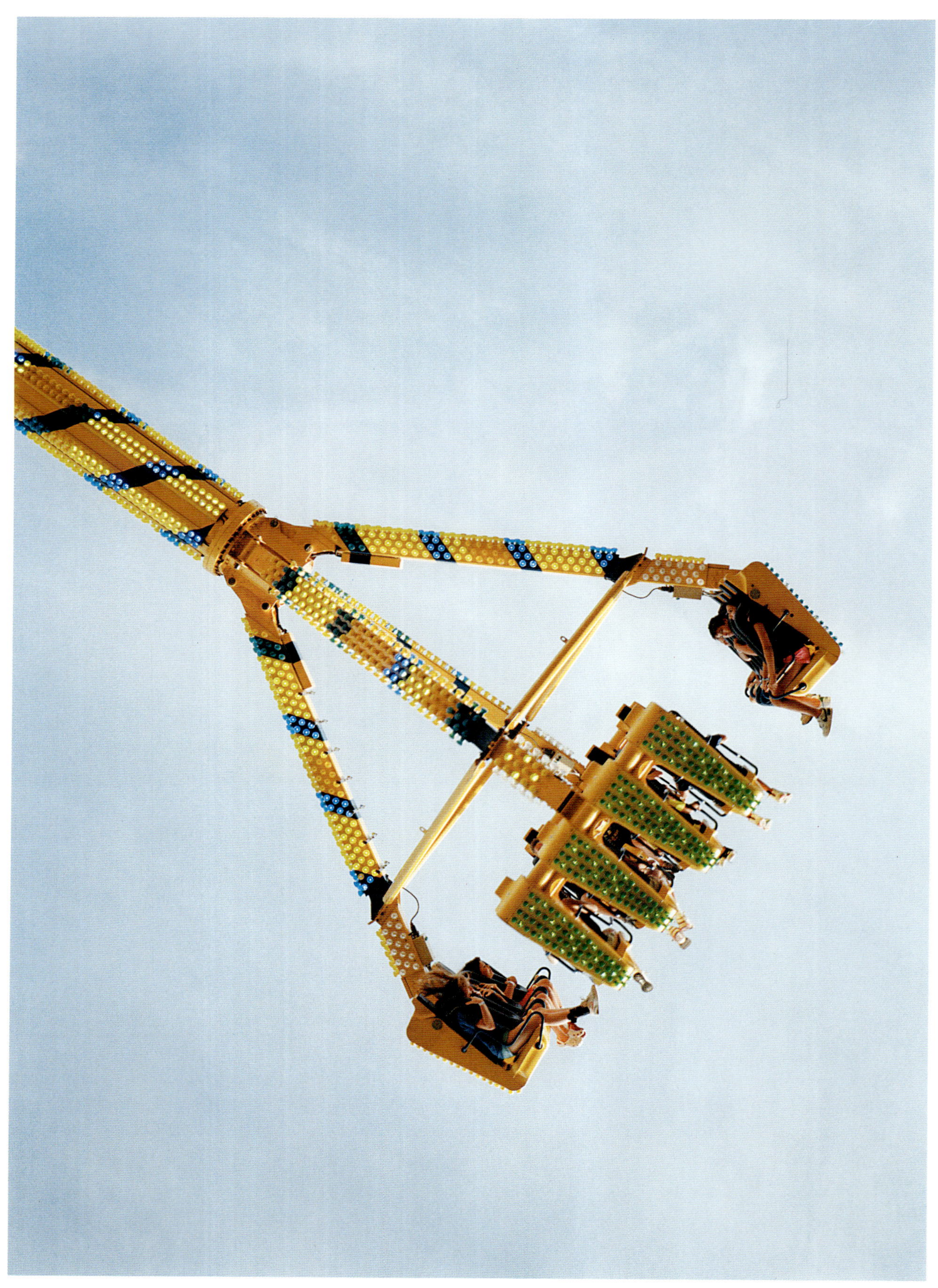

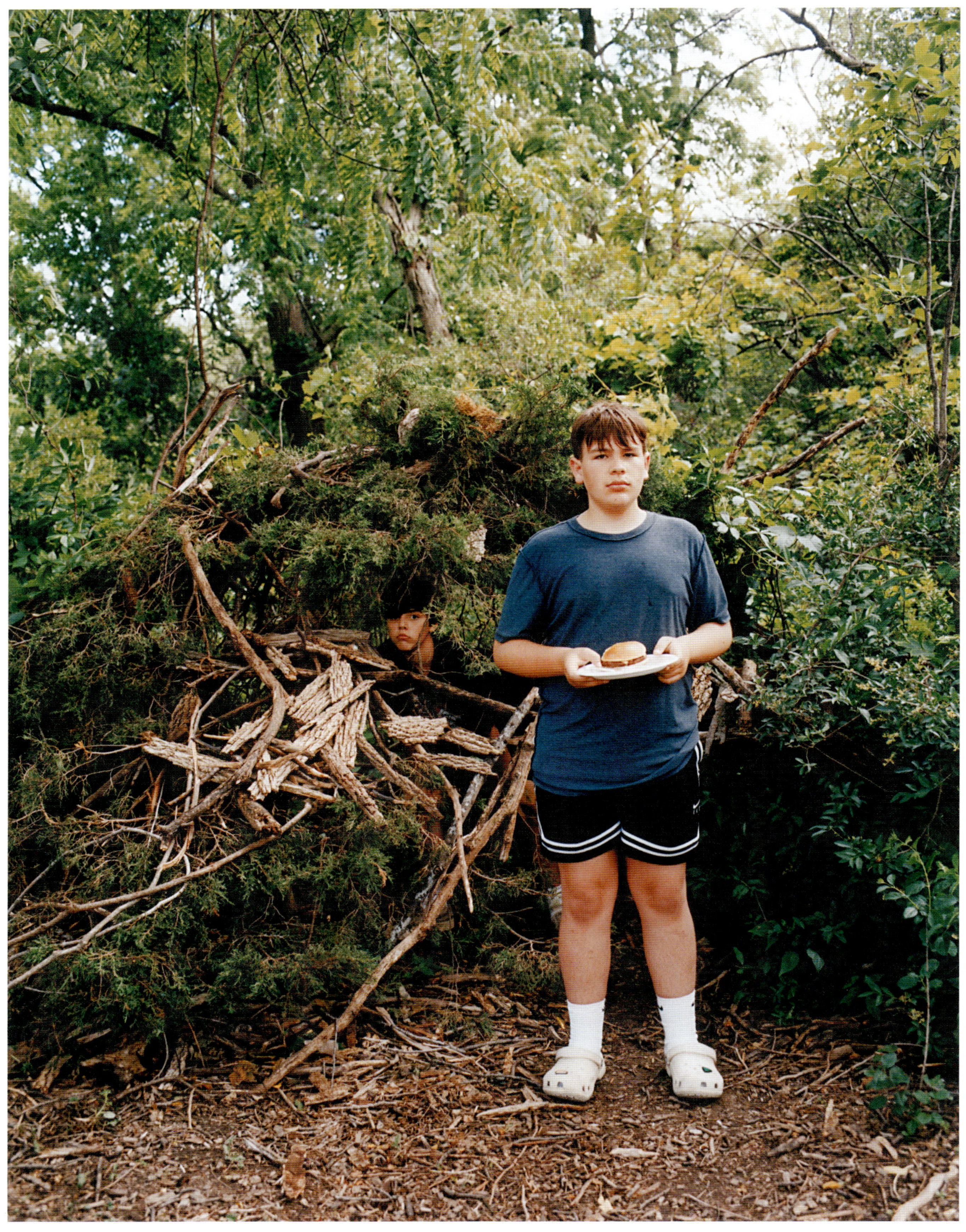

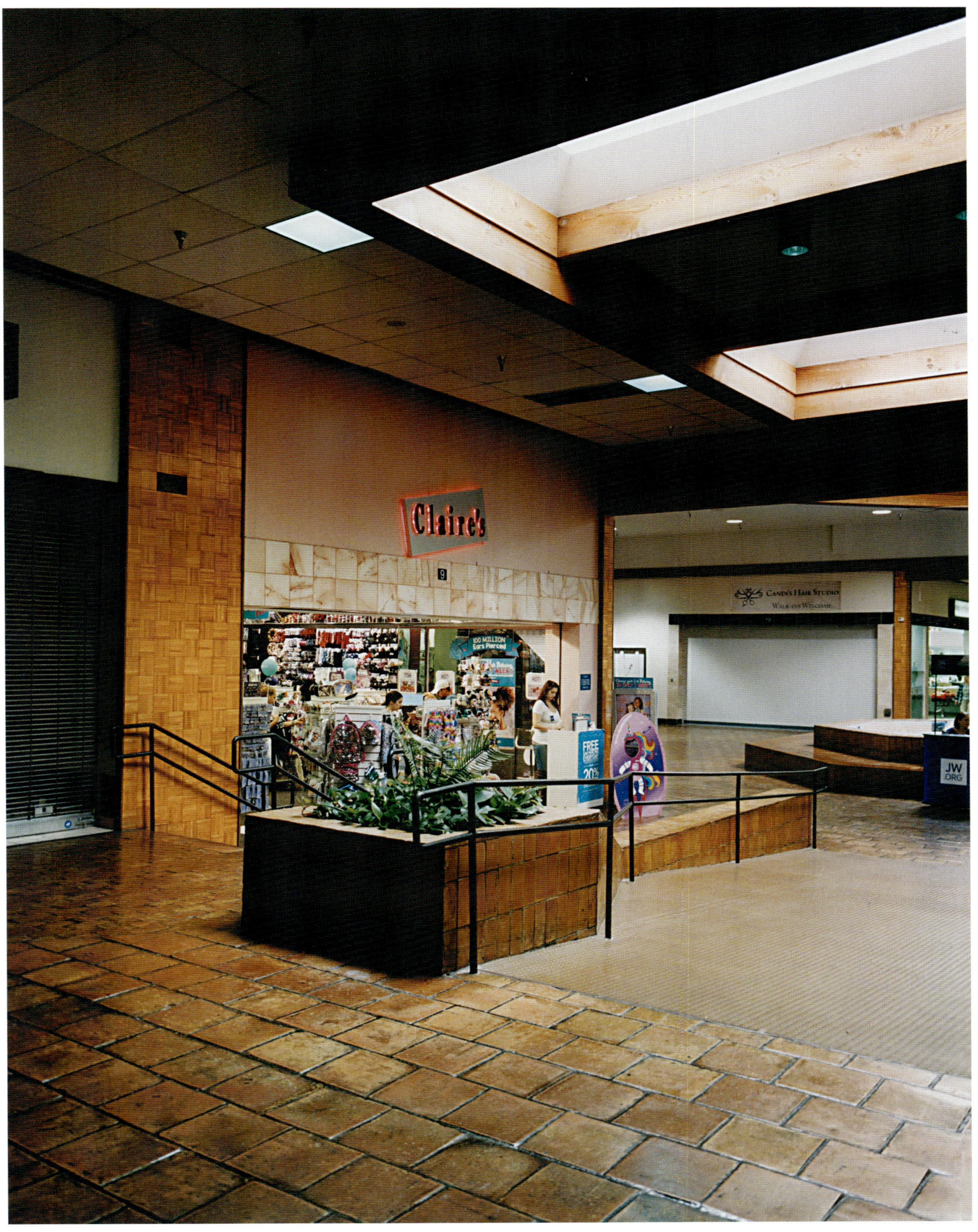
Claire's
9
100 MILLION
Ears Pierced
CANDI'S HAIR STUDIO
WALK-INS WELCOME
FREE
JW.ORG

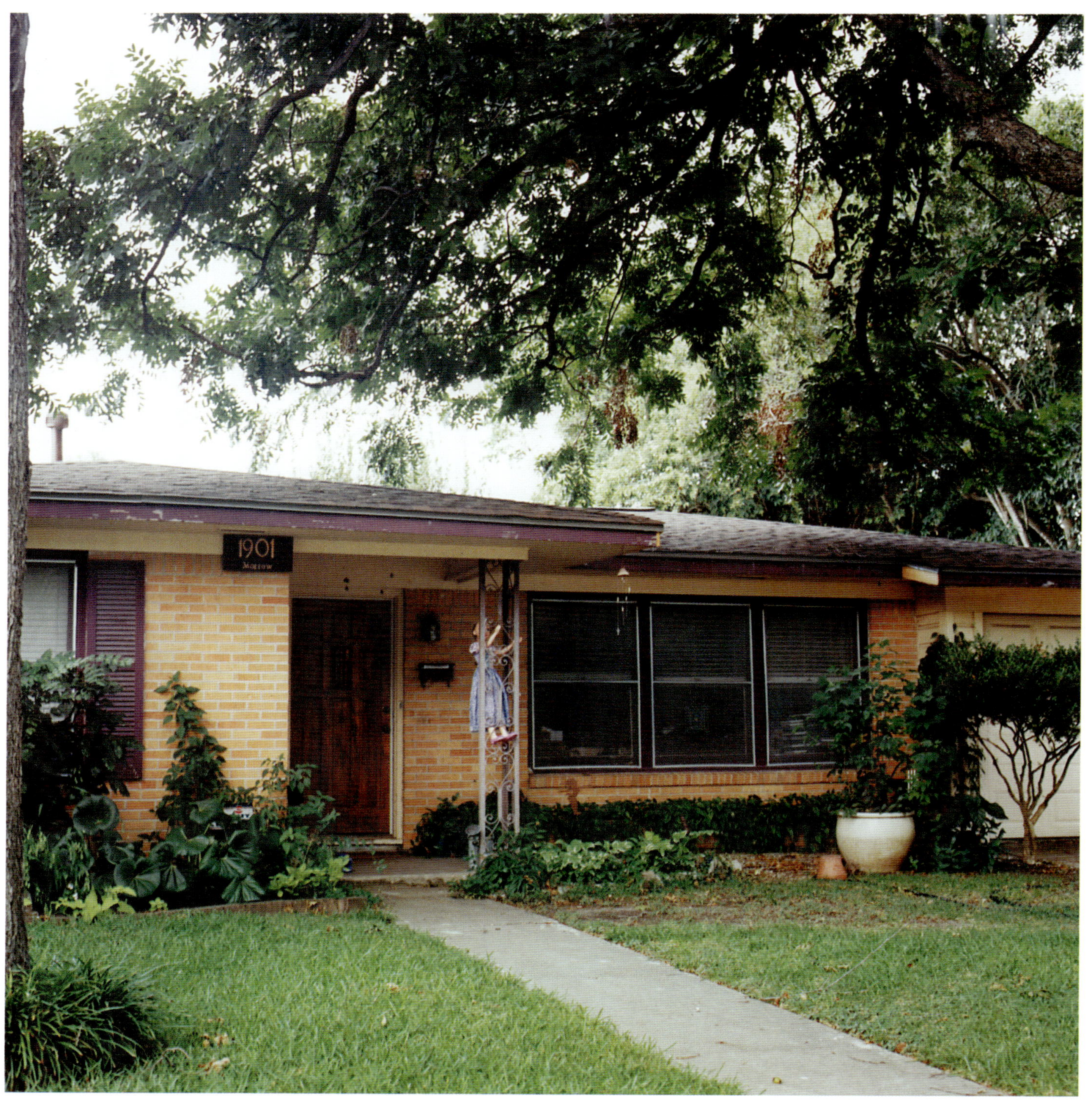
1901

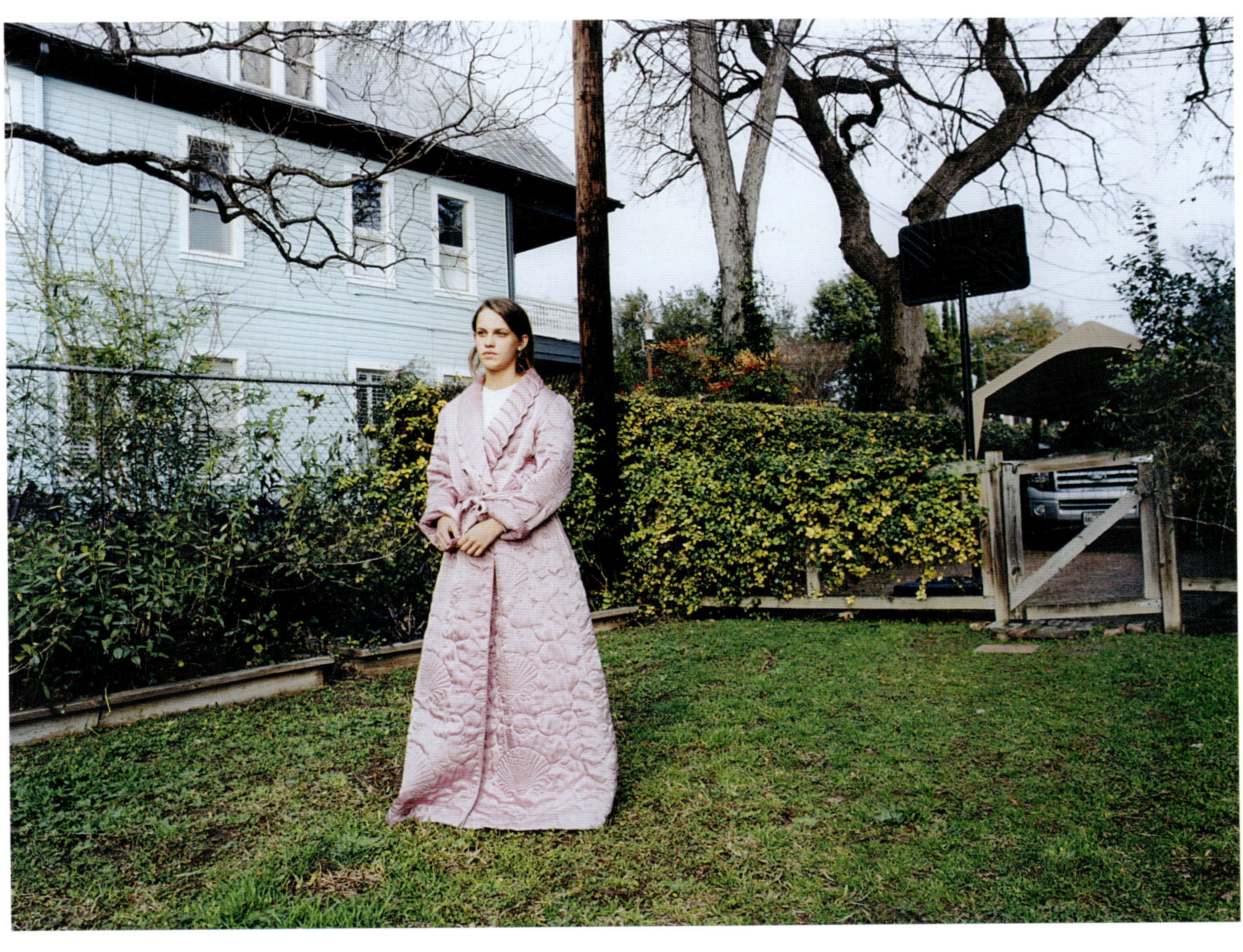

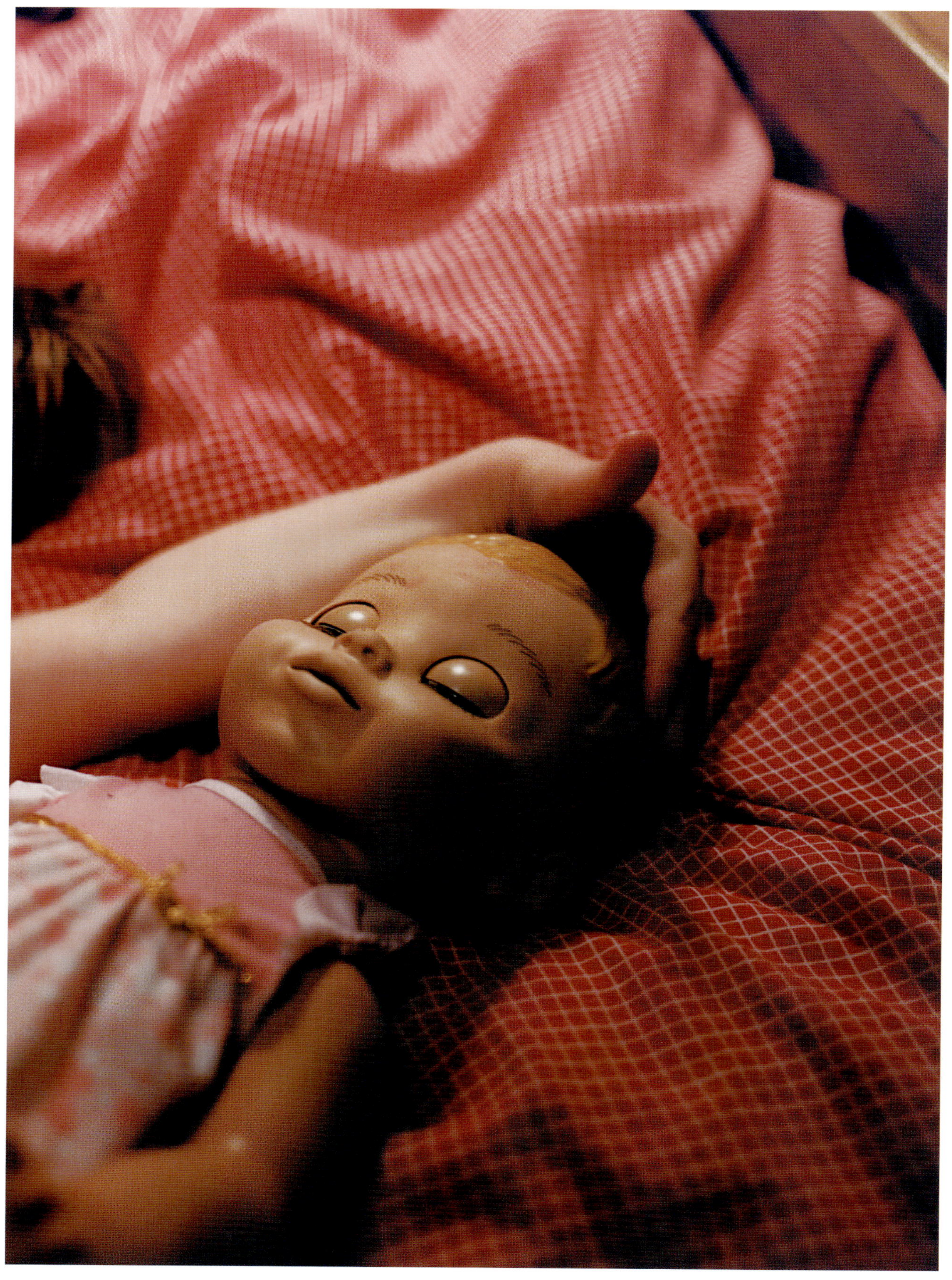

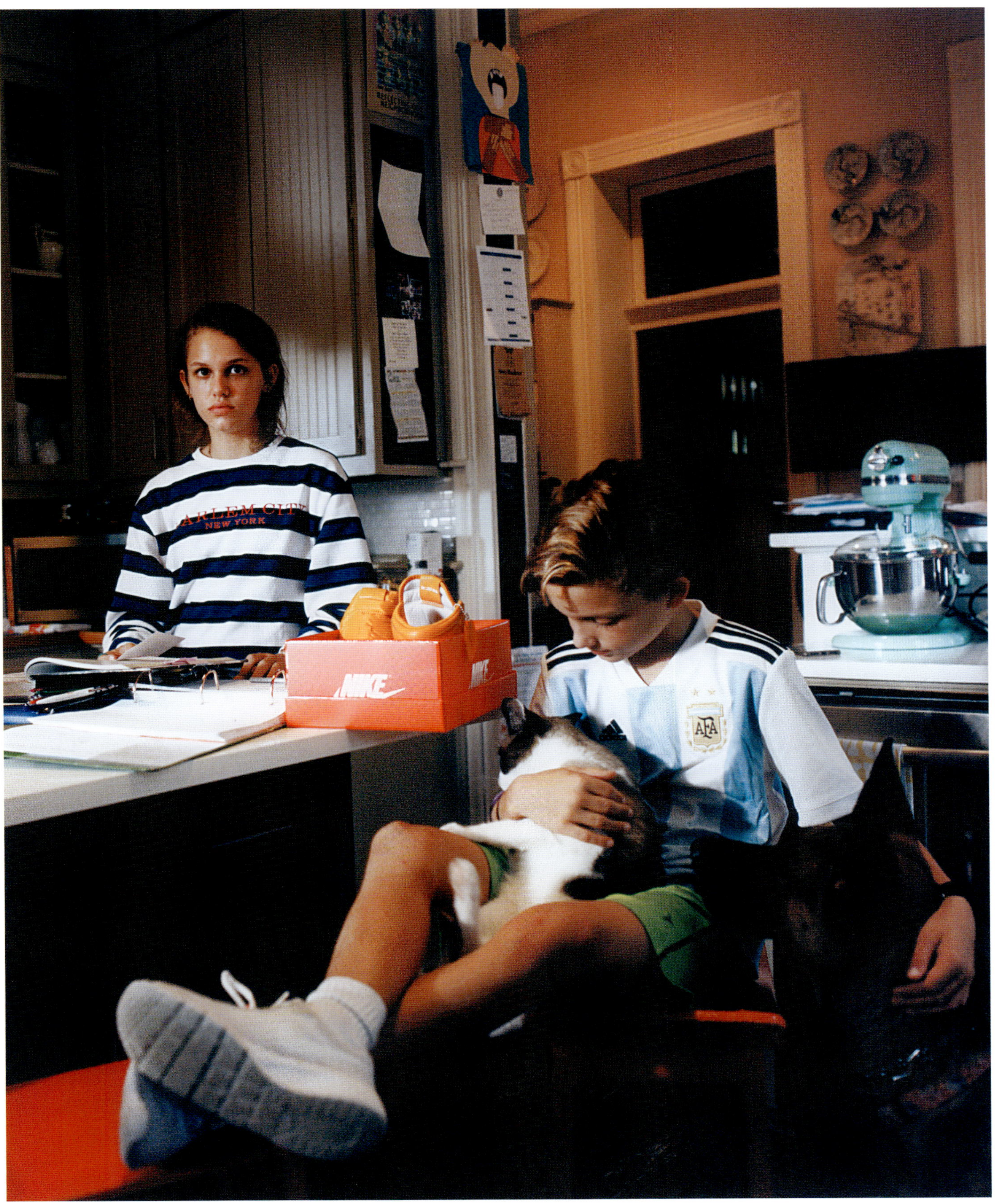
NEW YORK
NIKE
NIKE
AFA

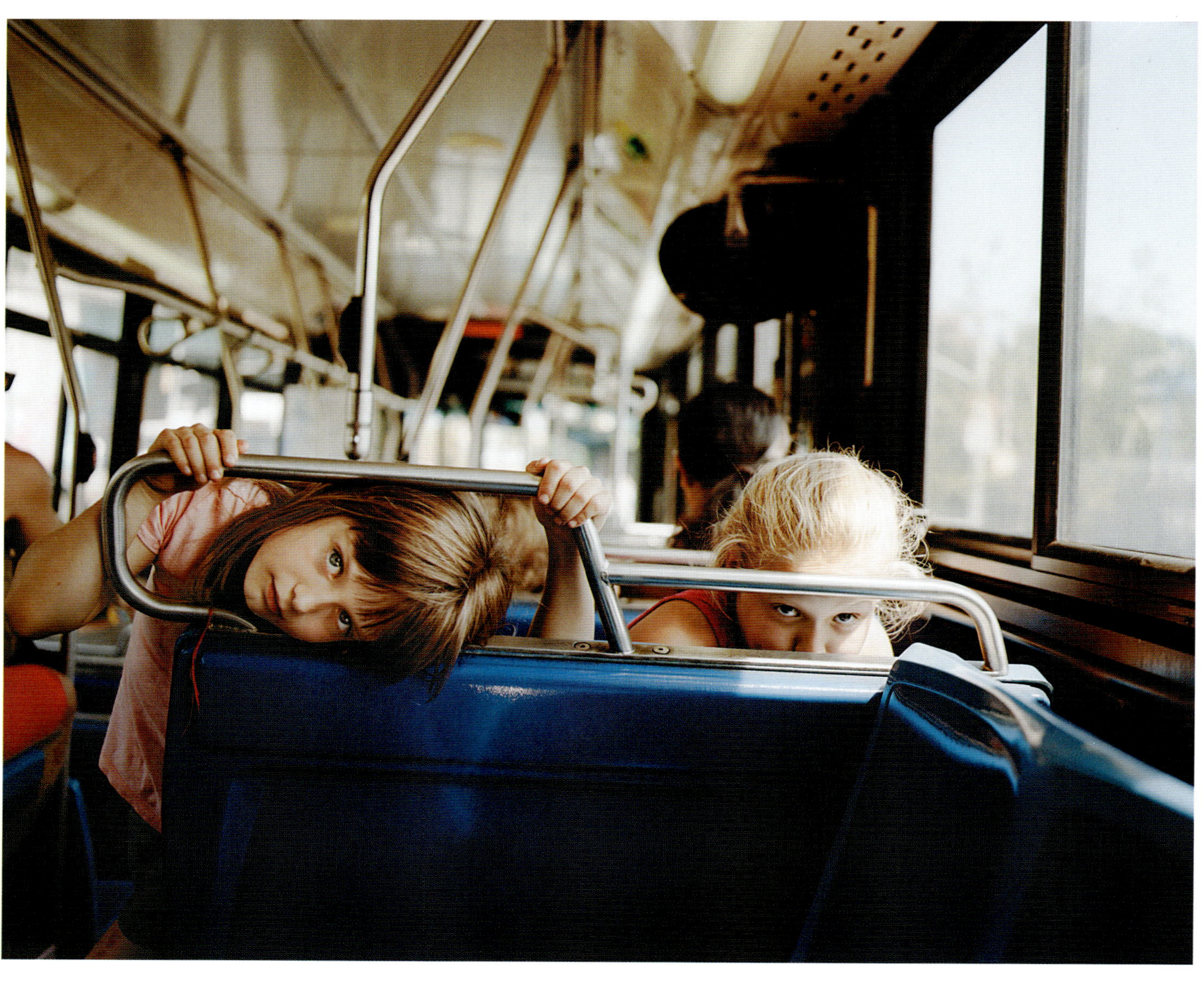

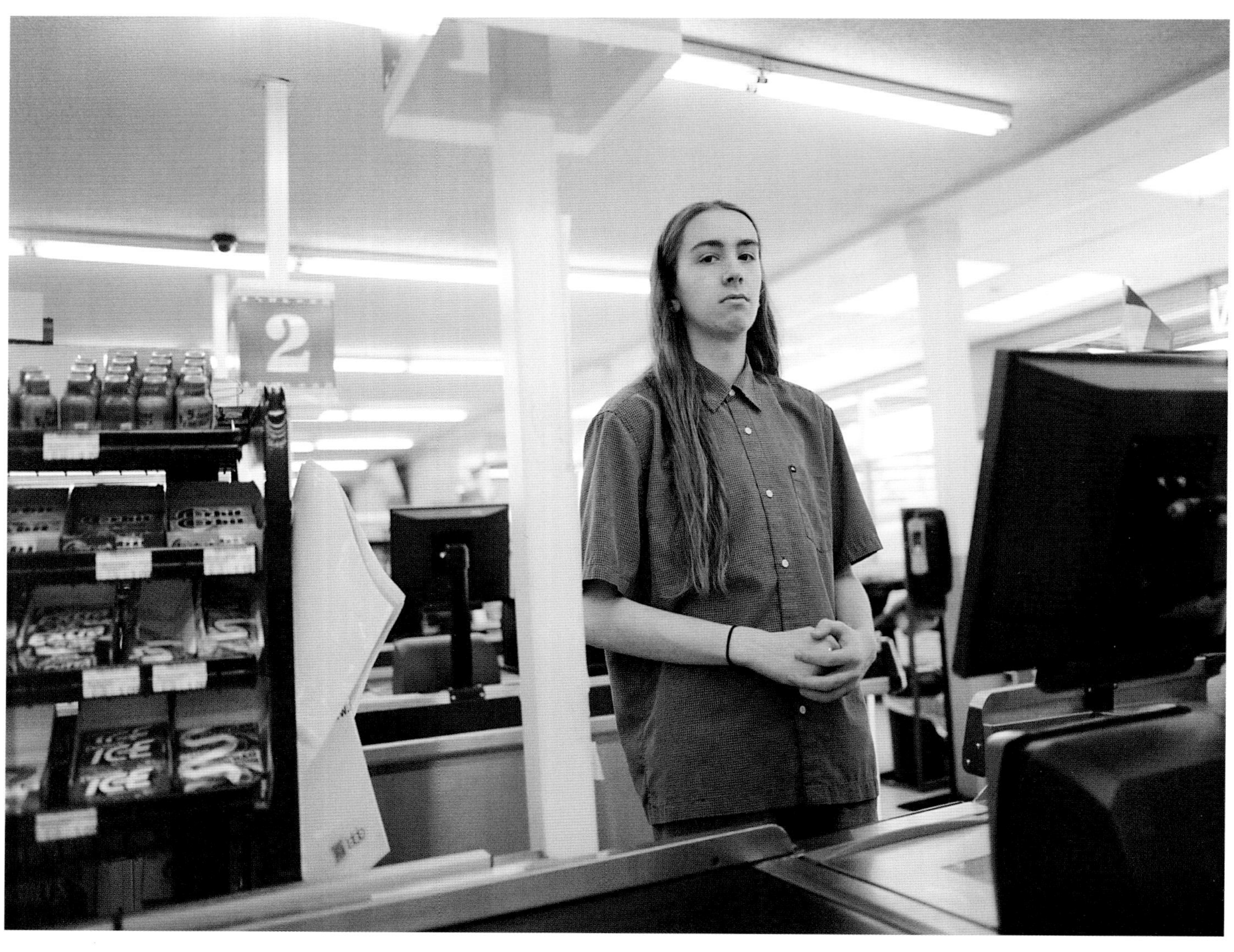
2
ICE
ICE

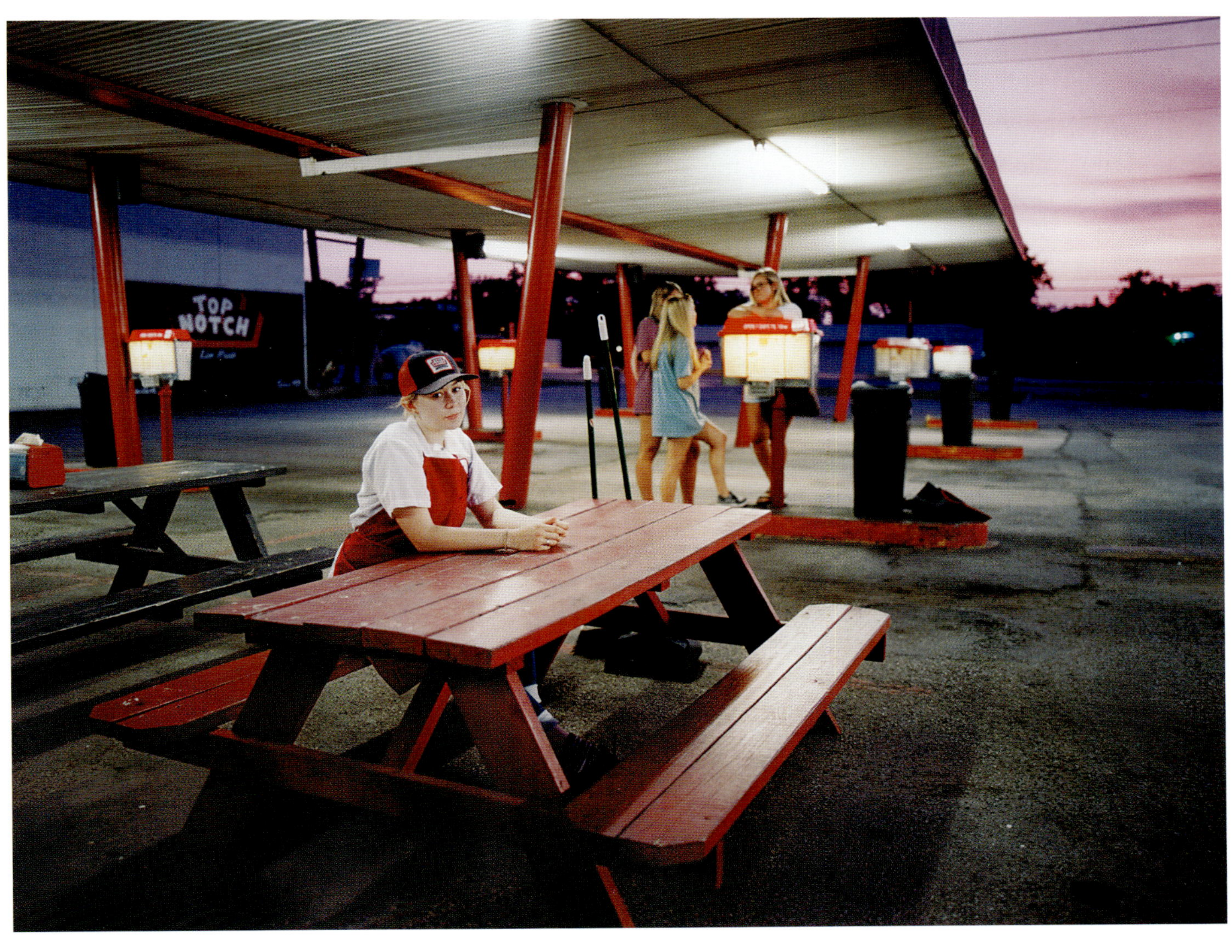
TOP
NOTCH

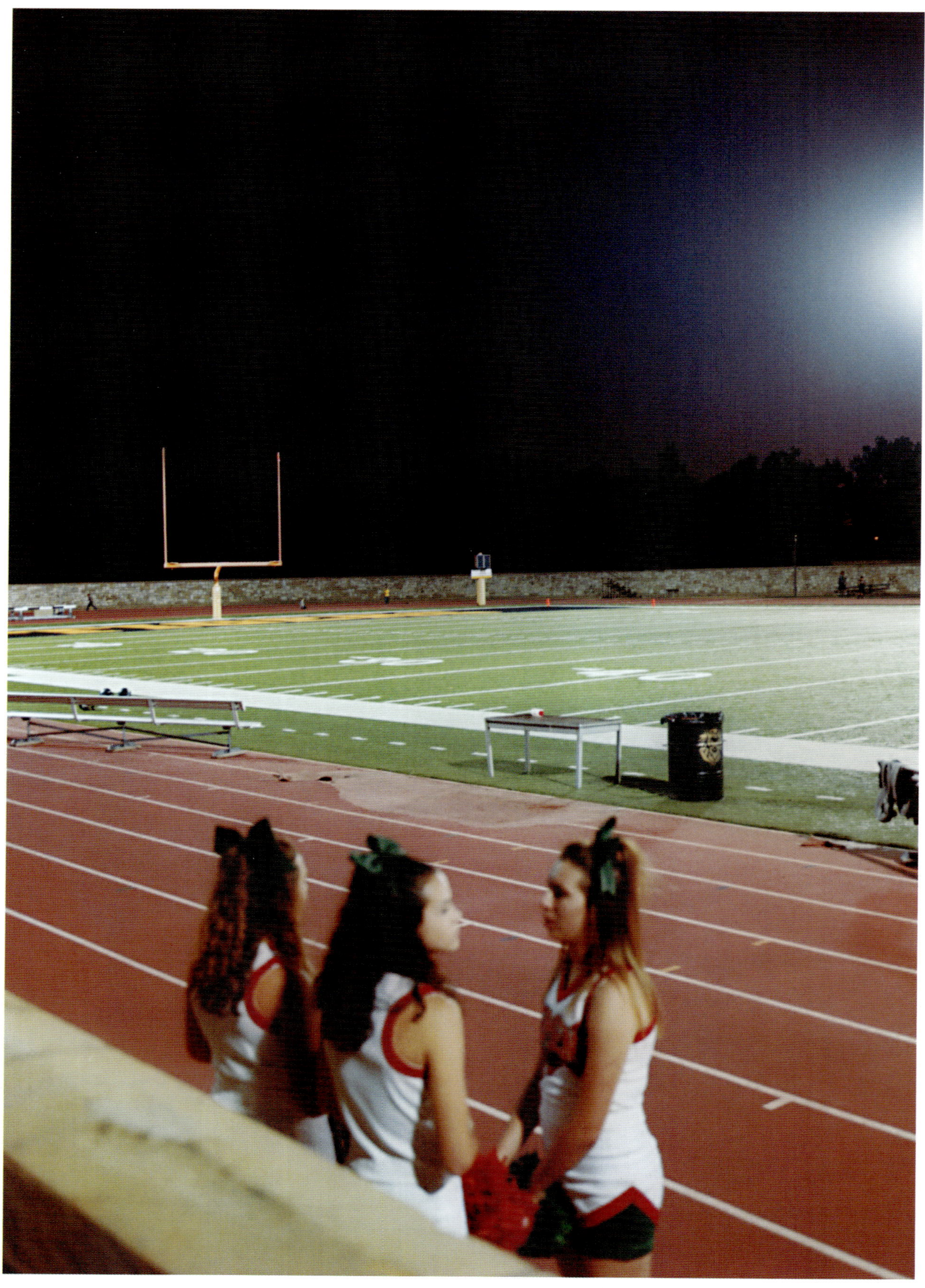

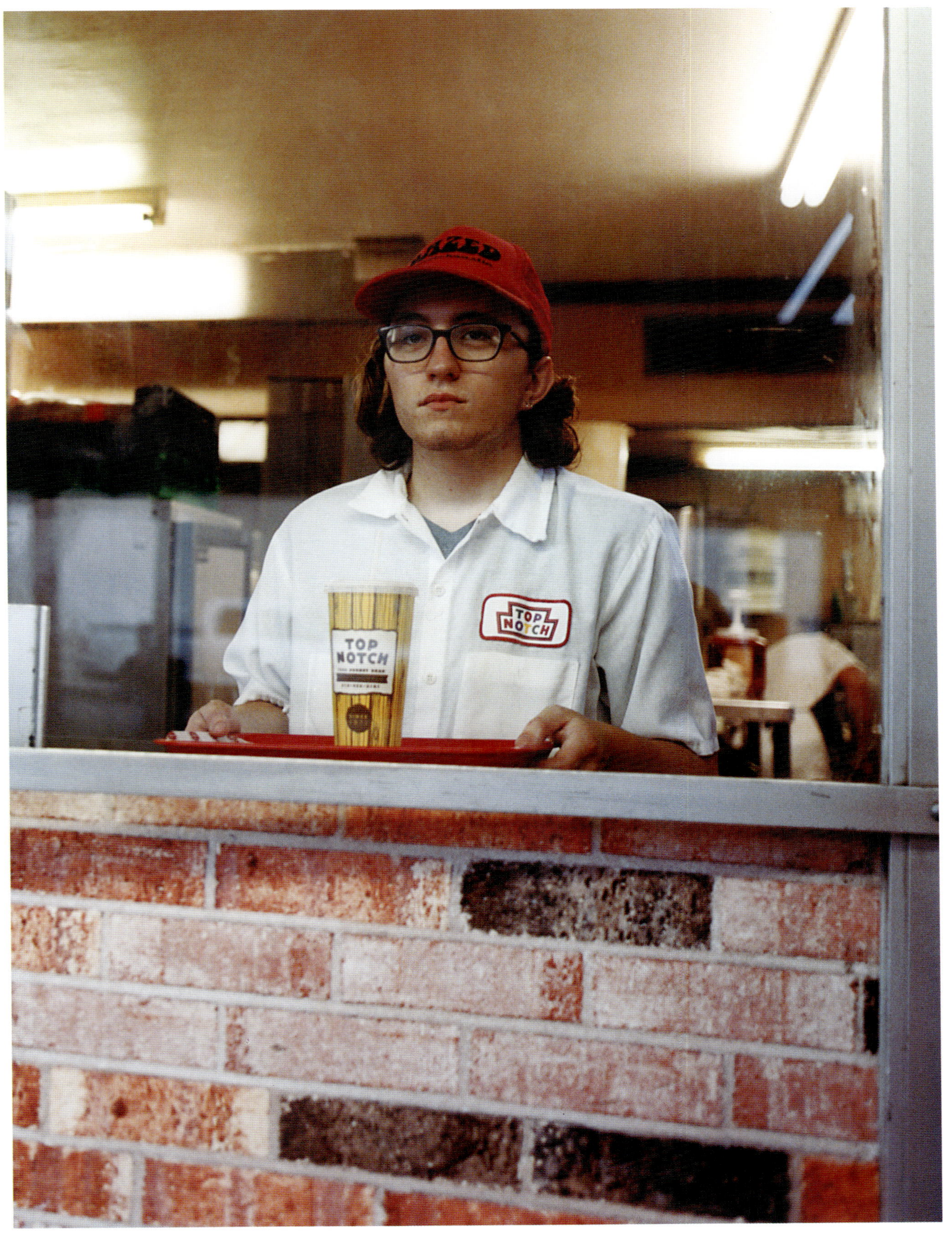
TOP NOTCH
TOP NOTCH

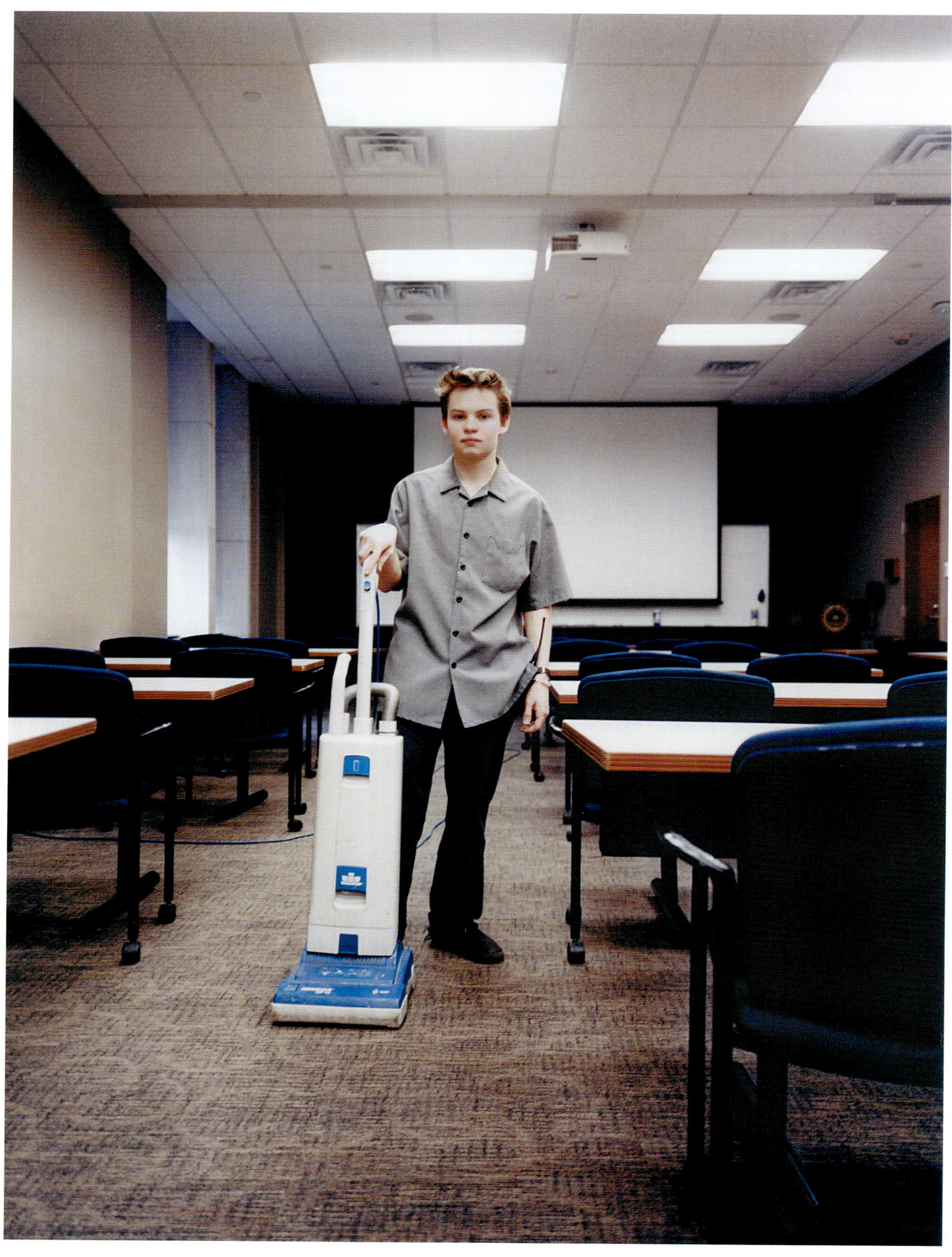

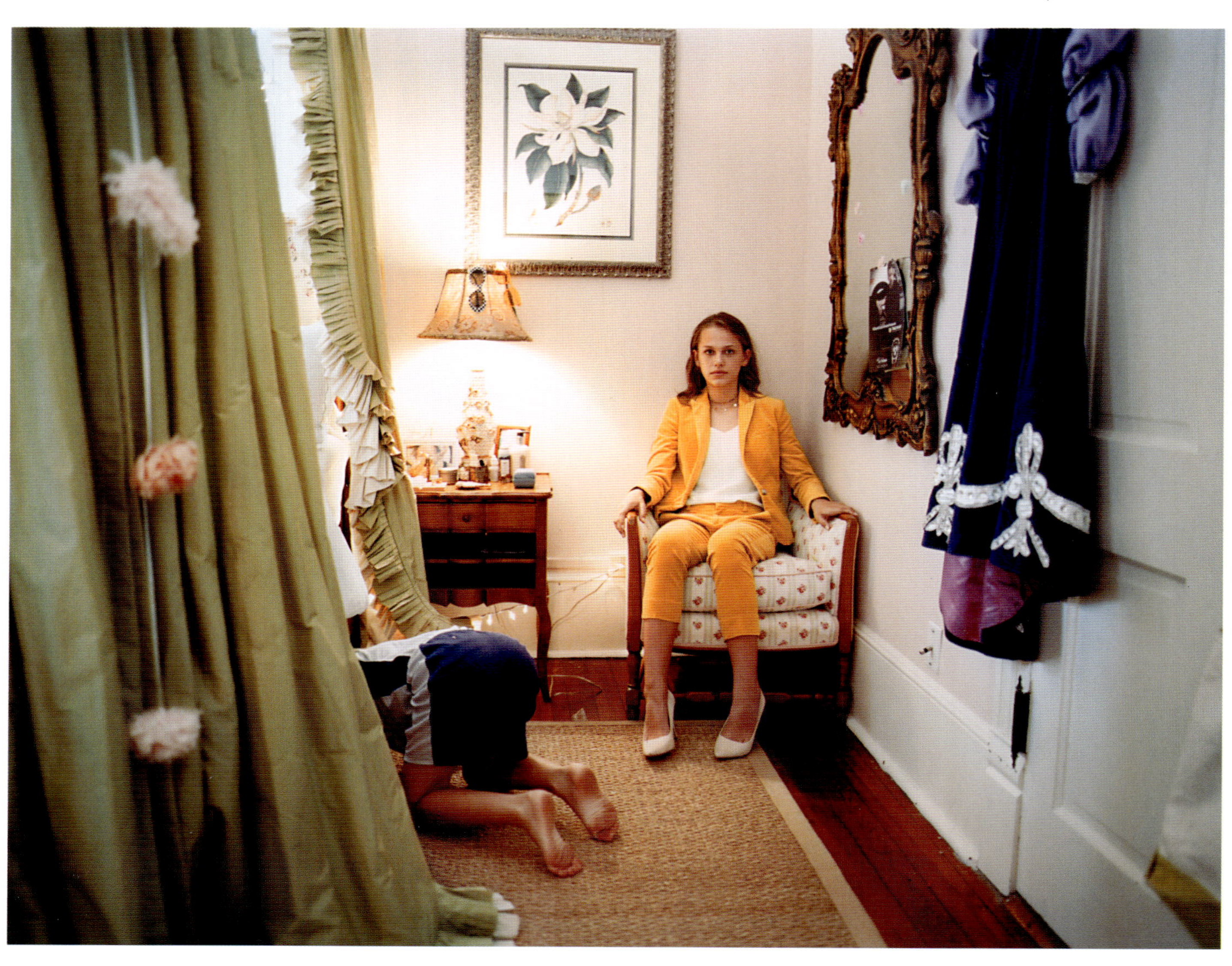

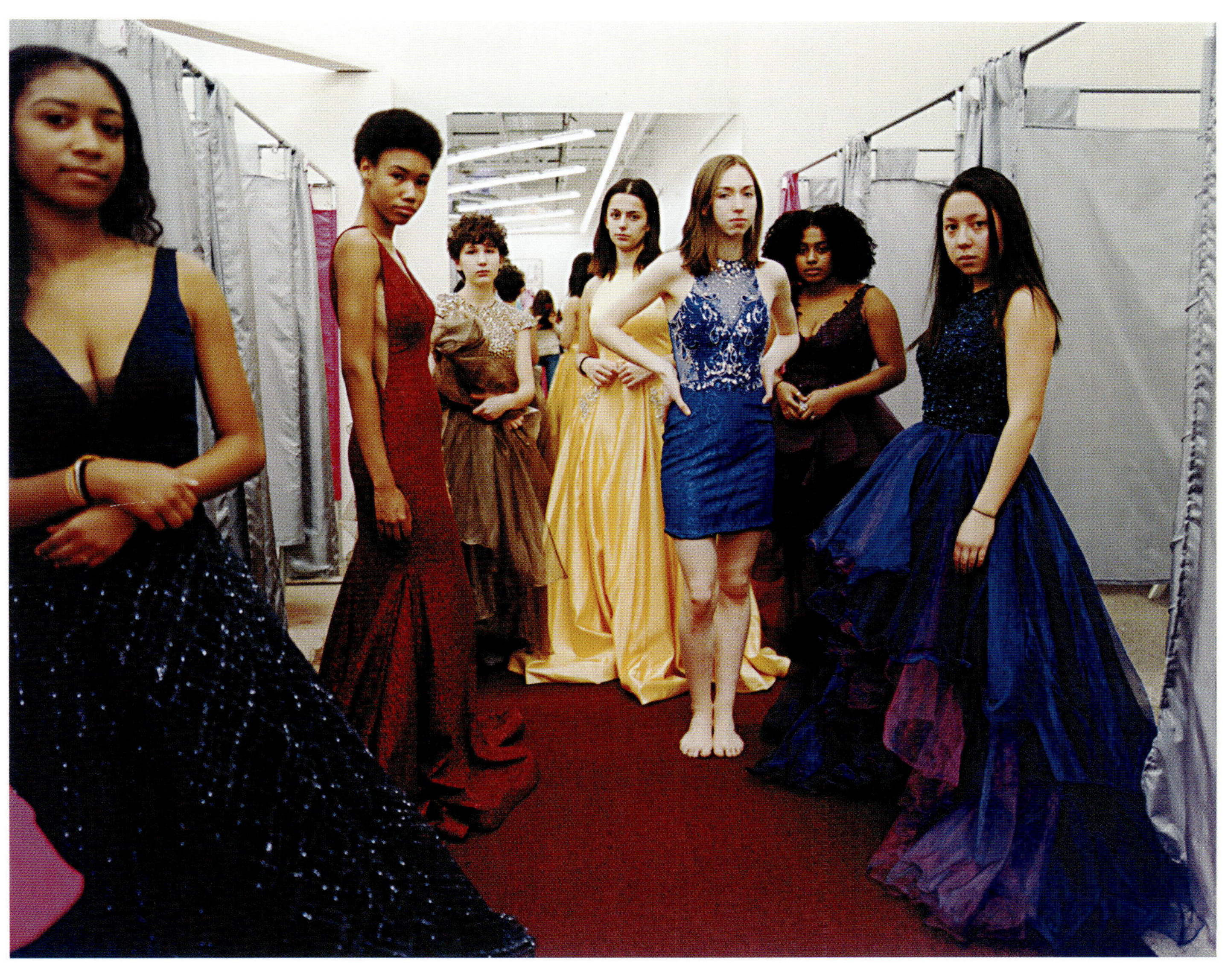

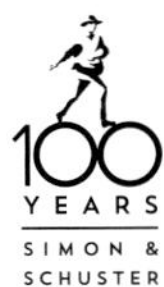

1230 Avenue of the Americas
New York, NY 10020

First Simon & Schuster hardcover edition November 2024

SIMON & SCHUSTER and colophon are registered trademarks of Simon & Schuster, LLC

Simon & Schuster: Celebrating 100 Years of Publishing in 2024

For information about special discounts for bulk purchases, please contact Simon & Schuster Special Sales at 1-866-506-1949 or business@simonandschuster.com.

The Simon & Schuster Speakers Bureau can bring authors to your live event. For more information or to book an event, contact the Simon & Schuster Speakers Bureau at 1-866-248-3049 or visit our website at www.simonspeakers.com.

Design: Roque Strew
Production Manager: Chau Nguyen

Printing and Scanning:
LTI Lightside Photographic Services, New York
My Own Color Lab, New York

Thanks to:

Chau and BJ
Katie Dunn
Nick Fiori
Gerard Franciosa
Justin King
Tarrah Krajnak
Anthony Maddaloni
Sean Manning
Dave McCary
Peter McGuigan
Carmen Pasquesi
August Pross
Kelly Reichardt
Mimi Slater
Emily Stone
Taylor Swift
Aleck Venegas
Mickey, Gus, Daisy, Katie, Mom, and Dad

Manufactured in China

1 3 5 7 9 10 8 6 4 2

Library of Congress Cataloging-in-Publication Data has been applied for.

ISBN 978-1-6680-3600-6
ISBN 978-1-6680-3602-0 (ebook)